NAVSSES

The Navy's Country Club of Scandalous Mannerisms of Waste, Fraud and Abuses

By Lawrence A Lueder

2009

Also By L. Lueder

A 1950s American Childhood in Morocco (Memoir)
Sunaru (Science fiction survival on a distant planet)

None of this book may be copied without explicit written authorization from the author.

ISBN:1-4392-1931-1
ISBN-13: 9781439219317

Visit www.booksurge.com to order additional copies.

TABLE OF CONTENTS

INTRODUCTION

I write this book for several reasons and to be more specific, I write this book to demonstrate some of the evil and corrupt ways that the NAVY operates when dealing with hardworking and honest personnel. This is about absolute power and how it can corrupt even the best of us. I will demonstrate how the NAVY squanders taxpayers monies, and how over time, the departments are heading towards an extremely obtuse pyramid of degrading intelligence. This is about the dummying down, if there is such a word, of NAVSEA/ NAVSSES. No one whom I knew brags about working at NAVSSES, and it just might be because, frankly, it doesn't sell. A good business sells itself.

None of what I write about or disclose could reasonable be classified to harm national security. Nothing in this book is about ship movements, status and or has anything to do about a Navy ship makeup or how it operates. And since government employees are all public servants, I can write about them as freely as the President's of the United States aids write books about the president and his cronies. NAVSSES and NAVSEA officials all get paid via tax dollars, and as such the taxpayers and citizens of the United Stated all have a right to know the truth about it ills.

This is about the lack of respect, fairness and dignity for all hardworking people working of the Navy and other similar military institutions. Even if there has to be different pay scales between the engineers and the technical engineers, accountants and others, I hope to demonstrate that there exists an-air of distrust between all working factions that are employed by the NAVY at NAVSSES. So while technicians and ex-secretaries promoted to technical positions via upward mobility, and are all doing exactly the same work, the Navy uses a phony and humiliating pay scale using illegal promotional practices. It's a phony bureaucratic organization in the sense that promotions aren't truly based on experience and knowledge of subject matter, they appear to be based on whether the supervisor/manager like's you.

Make no mistake; much of what I relay is applicable to all of the armed forces. And it's not just for the civilians that I write about; it also includes our military personnel. Originally, when I wrote the book, I included actual names, but I decided to omit them after a few people read it and felt it best to leave them out, or change them to protect the slimy creeps. So if some of the statements sound like you—it's you pal.

Per the Department of the Navy, Employees' Guide to the Standards of Conduct issued by the Assistant General Counsel (Ethics), 1000 Navy Pentagon, Washington, D.C. 20350-1000, (Presidential Towers [NC-1], Room 7000), January 2006, the management at NAVSSES violates many of the guides principles of Public Service. This book exposes many of the violations. The philosopher Plato once said, "The penalty for not monitoring the behavior of management is to be mismanaged and abused by people more sinister than themselves."

The bottom line of this book is to give voice to all those people who were and are still being wronged at NAVSSES and other similar military institutes. It was written to give these abused people some form of relief from an organization that still operates with blinders of the true and honest achievers.

RANTING

For those of you that might take offense to what I write about and will eventually rant when it sinks in that I wrote this book, because I was a sore loser, just remember this; I do this to show you that I am a better man for speaking up. You see; when you work for any of the military organizations there is an unwritten code that you should never speak negatively about your organization, and especially about your supervisors and managers. Most people retire with a knife in their heart from the hurt and the humiliation that the Navy places on them, and it's this reason why so many of them die an early death from keeping the festering knife in their sole. I won't let that happen to me – I'm stabbing back with this book of truth, so that I can continue to live with my head held up high, knowing that I did something about it.

Complainers about what I have to say you find will be much of the managerial types, the over paid and such.

I can't tell you of how many times that I wrote my name down on anonymous surveys the Navy kept issuing every year, in the hopes that the Navy was listening. But, nope, I never heard anything from them. At best, we would receive a glossed over report that indicated that we fell somewhere in the middle of the industry standard, for likes and dislike about work and our work environment. Hence, I wrote this book of truths.

If I mention or interject the way a certain person dressed, or I happen to include some of my own nit picking opinions about that person, I did so to get back at the managers and supervisors, who had no qualms about making fun of others around them at NAVSSES, especially making rude remarks about some of the subordinates. Therefore, I feel that if I had to hear condescending comments about others and or about me from the managers and such, regarding dress code, body odor and mannerisms, I should include my own about some of the buffoonish managers and supervisors, which I unfortunately met and or had to work under. I hate that phrase, to work under; it has that sexual connotation about it.

Anyway - some of my comments also relate to others I heard from, and once they discovered that I was writing this book, they all wanted to have some input. Unfortunate, many people complain about working conditions, few if any bother to take the time to write it down, to make it official. So while I heard from many complainers, about the horrific way that NAVSSES was being managed, few if any took the time to write it down, and send me the specifics. Most of them feared retaliation or loss of job from NAVSSES management if they spoke up. They were the silent victims.

For those people who did provide me with feedback for this book, I took the time to include highlights of their stories sprinkled throughout as samples, sans identifying the person. I might also include that ever since this book was published that I've heard from others, who were contemplating writing their own story.

The most common complaint, which I heard from NAVSSES employees, had to do with fifteen plus years or more of excellent service and repeatedly being overlooked during promotions, over the less experienced young people just out of college. And there were other stories…

Since this is my book, I may on and off throw in an offending brain scrambling metaphor in what might seem like an inappropriate interjection. By the way, whenever some big shot gave Michelangelo a hard time, Mike would paint a likeness of the person in his painting of heaven and hell, The Final Judgment. The pain in the ass person was depicted in hell, because God doesn't like hypocrites. This book is my Judgment of some of the management people from NAVSSES.

So as you read this I will reveal that the way the Navy operates, when it relies on NAVSSES, to resolve problems with one of its ships. It's basically like hiring an inexperienced carpenter, or plumber to fix a problem in your house.

Some of my writing may seem like it flows a bit jerky, and there may be some grammatical errors, just remember it's me doing all of the editing. I'm writing this as quickly as possible, least the Management draws a blank regarding what I am about to reveal. Also the order of the many subject matters may sound juxtaposed, but you'll get the jest of my book. Also - not relative to NAVSSES, I may include some fluff issues that I have with the two-face evil Saudi Government. Many of my letters to the editors of various newspapers have published my thoughts about the Saudis, and I've included some of them in this book. I did so to demonstrate that our government and its so-called Middle East experts are way off course in understanding the Arab/Middle East mentality. You'll understand – keep reading.

I should also mention to the English majors – thanks for your thoughts. In the end - who really cares, it's the message stupid.

VIETNAM

I hope to show too, that many of our military personnel die in combat because some idiot with a paper degree up the ladder of command, which includes people in Washington, are making irrational decisions. Decisions that ends up killing our men that could have been avoided. For instance, under Secretary of War McNamara, during the Vietnam War in the early sixties, many of our pilots were ordered to fly into enemy territory caring a single bomb. And it was all done so that some officer could claim x-number of phony sorties and thereby adding an extra bling to his bloody shirt. The bottom line in the Vietnam War was a bunch of assholes in Washington with zip war fighting experience dictating such stupidity, such as, the enemy shoots first or Hanoi is off limits to bombing. And the most criminal decision making of all, was to drop our boys in the middle of the jungle to defend for weeks at a time a mound of dirt, only to give it back to the enemy after a number of our boys were murdered defending a pile of garbage.

War is hell, and if you're in it, you shouldn't be picking who lives and who dies. War is not some chess game. The war in Vietnam could have been ended within the very first year it was started, simple by carpet-bombing Hanoi until the government totally surrendered. Fifty thousand young American men died because of a bunch of idiots — the same idiots that had our troops cut and run in the face of handful of jungle people time and time again.

In the war of Iraq, soldiers were riding in ridiculously designed Hummers. I say ridiculous, because it was obvious that some ex-civilian or commander, that was once in charge of issuing contracts to build them had retired from working for the Army or Marines, and continued to work as a contractor to build the overpriced piece of junk Hummer. Anyone that is supposed to understands explosives, and the effects of explosives is elementary; they should know that you never design a vehicle with sides perpendicular or horizontal to the ground. And that's exactly how the crappy Hummers were designed. About the best the Hummers were designed to do is to patrol the street of Camden, New Jersey, the city labeled the most violent in America. The so-called engineers of the Hummer should go to jail for all the deaths that they have caused from designing such a ridiculously overpriced crafted vehicle that was not fit to be used in a war zone.

Which brings me to this. While our soldiers were fighting in Iraq with inferior bulletproof vests, NAVSSES was finding money to hand out $7000 plus awards and more to its managers and above, including annual pay raises.

In the Iraq war Marines were ordered to stand down in the town of Falugha, a terrorist stronghold, before the Marines were allowed to finish off the terrorist, which eventually caused countless numbers of Marines to be killed. Sure the Marines were allowed to return to finish the fight, but only after the Iraq army demonstrated that they were pansies when it came to fighting. Time after time, American military men die because of some person with a piece of paper with no hands on experience is making life and death decisions, and it needs to stop. Colin Powel was another one of those idiot commanders that stopped the initial war before the Iraqi elite guards were totally annihilated. I just knew that many of our young boys would later die from attacks by the Iraqi Army. People of the Middle East, basically Muslims, do not in any way play honorable – witness the suicide bombers and decapitations.

Typical newspapers often label the war bungling mistakes as, bureaucratic refusals to supply, the best equipment led to the troops deaths. And there's the bungling by the Army of a Blackman who re-enlisted seven times using seven different identifications. At his last enlistment, the Army put him in charge of security. His name was David Piccard. Actually, it wasn't his real name, because he had several names. Piccard was just one of them. He must have picked up that name from the television series Star Trek. How's that for military security?

Forget Piccard and all the other stuff and think about this for a second. Two major shipyards presently contain the bulk of all Navy ships. One is in the East coast and one is in the West coast. Is the Navy setting us up for another round of Pearl Harbor attack revisited? One nuke bomb in a suitcase going off at any one of the major Navy shipyards, and none of the ships will be fit to deploy from radioactive contamination.

Hopefully, this book should make the Navy and other military institutes make better decisions and not rely on the inexperienced paper tiger mentality. And I hope to rein in the outrageous pay scales, and benefits that the Navy presently pays out to the inexperienced and such phony engineers, which consider themselves untouchable elitist. Elitist that behave as Nazis, obsessed towards repressing technicians by rounding them up in their midst to rid of them, or cause them harm via unequal pay scales and awards.

I add this piece so as to calm down those who might feel justified in some pseudo retaliations for my book. It comes from an article that I believe was written by Christopher Cavas, April 20, 2007 in the Navy Times. In the article regarding various Inspections and Survey known as InSurvs of three Mid-Life Ships, The cruiser USS Chosin, the USS Stout and the USS Pearl Harbor, were all found to be unfit for combat operations.

Several of the Captains went on to say that, "The number of discrepancies is disturbing and that there is enough commonality between the ships to make him think there's an endemic problem in the force. The scale of the deficiencies, spread across all of the ship's departments, suggest that there is a severe and long-standing problem with low standards; low initiative in finding/fixing/managing problems and following up on documented problems; poorly managed programs; and an apparent inability to train junior people in material management. All that even though there is plenty of funding."

And then there's this article I recently read in the newspapers regarding seventeen senior Air Force officers that were disciplined, including a three-star general in charge of logistics, for poor oversight in the shipment of nuclear warheads to Taiwan. The discipline included six Air Force generals, nine colonels and two Army colonels. September 26, 2008. How many more of these types of bungling are the public going to put up with from overpaid paper tigers? This is what happens when people you know get promoted over the people that know.

Ok, I'll admit that some of what I just presented had nothing to do with NAVSSES, but that's your opinion. I say it's the same only on a different scale. People at NAVSSES may not be dying, not that anyone can see, but if you were to read some of the comments the employees write in the surveys about working conditions and incompetent managers and or supervisors...

MY BACKGROUND

But first I have to give you a little background about myself, and something about the Navy's pay scale. Much about how I was hired for the Navy you can read about in one of my books titled Mom's Chicken House. In it, I describe how I applied for the Navy Shipyard apprenticeship program back in 1969. I go into some detail about the people, and the ups and downs of how I was constantly striving to better myself for the next promotion, which never materialized, hence this book.

So, here I was working in an apprenticeship as a tool and die-maker for the Philadelphia Navy Shipyard. Basically, tool and die-makers were considered the crème of the machinist industry, the elite working with tolerances +.0001 of an inch. We were picked because of our higher scores on the entrance exams, to be accepted into the apprenticeship. Initially when I applied at the Shipyard, I asked to work in the electronics department since I had a vast knowledge on the subject, from building radios and transmitters when I was a child. Anyway, I relished every moment during those heydays of shipbuilding. I was fortunate enough to get my hands on just about every type of mechanical machinery with never a waste of time. I was so confident in my field and then some, to where I was teaching some of the old salts new tricks and shortcuts on equipment that they had been using for years.

Mechanical tinkering was second nature to me. Ever since I can remember as a child and long before I was hired at the shipyard, I had amassed a vast knowledge of mechanical contraptions. In a way, you could say that I had far more knowledge about electrical and mechanical components than a student could learn from any MIT University. I not only had hands on experiences of mechanical and electrical parts, I had book learning expertise from researching the components. At times, whenever I didn't have access, or the money to purchase the parts I needed to compete a project, I made my own electrical motors, and I made my own electrical components such as diodes, capacitors and wound my own electrical chokes. But the tool and die making was new and in a way, much of it came easy to me.

I was always an explorer of anything and everything you might say, a tinker. I liked the tool making place so much, that I often arrived long before it was time to start work. On a couple of severe weather condition days, I battled the heavy snowed over roads using wheels chains, only to find the shipyard closed. Summers were sweltering inside the all-metal buildings that we worked in, and during the winter long-John's helped fray off some of the cold, along with eight to twelve cups of coffee.

In the beginning, 1969, when I was introduced to the machinery world as an apprentice, I was given the initial task of converting a warehouse of the original tool shelves, filled with every cutting tool imaginable covered in Cosmo-lean grease, and ten years of dust, to the new drawer cabinet units. Let me just say that the first year, I arrived at work looking like a typical 1940s auto worker, and I went home that evening looking like a 1940s coalminer. Sitting anywhere was not allowed since it looked unprofessional, but my boss was lenient enough to know when to look away from time to time.

Anyway, there was nothing I couldn't manufacture out of a hunk of steel, from a precision cutting die to a complex contoured turbine blade. I lost count of how many beneficial suggestions I submitted, it was anywhere from eight to a dozen, most of them were complex special tools I designed and produced for specific jobs. Submitting suggestions, keeping an excellent leave record, volunteering to tackle the toughest jobs and so on, was suppose to help when it came to picking the next supervisor – but it wasn't happening.

What am I not doing right? I'll have to try harder. What next, the only way that I understood that you could get ahead in the machinery world (so I thought) was to take some college courses in business management. And that's exactly what I did.

Year after year, I signed up for as many courses that I could at Gloucester County College and took the courses. If you've never done this, let me just say that it was a grueling experience. You leave your job that ended at 4:00pm and rush to get to your classes at the college. Classes often ended around 10:00pm, which didn't leave much time to wind down in the evening. And I'm not even going to mention my dysfunctional family members, which I had to deal with since Dad passed away. Dad by the way left Mom holding the bag with three young boys; the oldest at the time was eleven years old. You got it, I was stuck helping Mom raise three boys until they could get on their own. And I'm not going to go into all the problems my ex-girlfriend was feeding me, besides her two children. And I'm not going to go into all the repairs my house required just to make it livable. You can read about it in one of my other books.

There is one other issue that isn't mentioned, whenever someone takes it upon himself to get ahead in life, by taking college courses above and beyond their regular work schedule. It's the coworkers; their attitude towards that person suddenly takes on an air of subtle negativity and jealousy. Again, I'll mention that you can read about it in my other book.

So, after all those classes and degrees that I finally received, I was hoping to qualify for a supervisor's position in the machinery world. But nope: some other kid that was popular with the boss was more in tune with getting promoted. Here was a kid just out of the military with little tool-making experience against my ten years, and it was obvious whom they wanted. Since this new young man was less experienced in the field, it was best that he get promoted, to where his function was more to delegate verses producing a tangible useful object. The guy was popular with everyone, and he tended to clown around too much. Too much so, that one night when he tried clowning around at a bar, the bar's bouncer crashed his head in with a bottle–killing him.

OK, now what? Well, what happened at about that time was that I was called to go work for the Design Division. Ok, I'm out of the shop, and I'm working in an office environment, white shirts and a tie were mandatory. There in Design, I must have worked just about every aspect of the various ships systems from hydraulics to propulsion. There was nothing or any system I could not handle and run with it. At home I was totally rebuilding car engines, I even built one of the first solid-state ignition system. And when Volkswagen started using fuel injectors in cars, I built my own for an older four cylinder Rambler.

So besides all that, what was I to do to get ahead in Design, the only people getting promoted were those with an engineering degree? So, back to college I went, only this time I needed engineering courses. Actually, I really gotten to like the tough mathematical challenges, and I strived to maintain high grades as usual. I took all that I could relating to engineering from Gloucester County College, and I took all that I could from Camden County

College and then I took some at Drexel University. By the way, I was paying for my own classes unlike many of the employees working at the Shipyard and at NAVSSES, which had their courses reimbursed?

At one point during some of my work in the Design Division I was asked by Public Works to redesign two fire fighting caissons for the SLEP program. That was a multi-million dollar program to refurbish some aircraft carriers. The caissons would be used for fighting fires on the carriers should anything serious breakout. The construction of the caissons needless to say was a major undertaking, which required supervising multiple shops from welders to pipe and electric divisions. The end result of the construct were two floating barge like structures with two 400 horsepower water pumps. The pumps would take water from the Delaware River and pump it to the carriers' flight decks when required. I designed, engineered and managed the complete construction of said caissons with electrical schematics, plumbing, structural and floatation design. And for all that Herculean superintending work, I received not even a thank you. Where was my promotions, or my bonus? Onward…

And then suddenly for real, the shipyard was in the process of closing. What now? Thankfully, I was transferred to NAVSSES. The feeling of being saved from unemployment from a decent paying job is indescribable. Before even getting a job at the Shipyard, long before that, I worked the fields with migrant workers getting paid by the basket filled with fruit or vegetable. While Dad was stationed in Montana, I worked my summer bucking hay bales for $6.00 a day. When Dad was transferred to North Dakota, I worked my summer in the wide-open fields, with migrant Mexican workers, hoeing quarter mile rows of sugar beets under the scorching sun. Then we moved to New Jersey, where once again, I found work working along side of migrant workers, from Puerto Rico, in the peach and tomato fields, where I was paid a quarter for each basket picked.

From working under the sun everyday, I finally got a job working indoors. I went on to work as an orderly in a nursing home. Bedpans, colostomy bags, bedsores and the whole gamut of assisting the super elderly became second nature. I worked in one nursing home after another and a couple of hospitals—none of them paid much more than minimum wage. Oh, I must not forget – I also watched over some thirty odd mentally ill patients at a mental institute too. So, you can see that a meaningful job with the government with all kinds of medical benefits and a retirement meant an awful lot to me.

Therefore, while reading this, make no mistake, I truly understand how some of the guys feel that were in my predicament of becoming unemployed, and then being saved from layoffs to working in an office atmosphere. Which explains why many of the technicians were very reluctant to speak up whenever they were insulted by the higher ups at NAVSSES and more.

SHIPYARD CLOSING

The shipyard closing followed by the massive unemployment was all based on the whims of some ghostly person in Washington. My feelings were there too, worried about whether or not I was going to be called to work for NAVSSES, after placing what seemed like one hundred applications. In the end, it was truly a blessing to know that I was called to work for NAVSSES. And then going back to visit old friends at the shipyard who were left behind was heartbreaking, it was as if I was floating on a cloud of security, while they were below me with hands raised up to be saved. The layoff of so many talented workers was not pretty. Depression, suicides and more followed the closing of the shipyard; the Navy has no idea of how many people that it was responsible for murdering.

Oh yeah, the Navy paid for some training on how to write a seventh grade resume, and there was some other minor training stuff, that they supplied in the hopes that it would help the unemployed find another job. But, we all know that the trainings were just a white wash to quickly close down the Shipyard as soon as possible. The training courses were elementary at best, fit to make a caveman giggle. It was people at the top making decisions for the people on the front line. Rather than talking directly with the people, the man at the top was a coward, pretty much like our director was at NAVSSES. It always baffled me as to how a director or superintendent could make so much money, and rarely if ever they visited the people that worked under them.

OUR DIRECTOR

Yep, our director at NAVSSES even admitted to us once that he hated to speak in public in front of a crowd. So why was he even promoted to such a prestigious position, I ask? It's not the guy at the top that makes great decisions or comes up with solutions, after all, how can he, when the bulk of his time is spent massaging his retirement to come, the Padding the Nest Syndrome. Face it; you people that worked at NAVSSES know that it's true.

Businesses and Industry to survive need to take risks, try new things, look beyond the self-almighty and others. Employees like myself with a slew of ideas and they knew it, I was ignored for fear of upsetting the management security blanket, the going through the daily motions mud heads. What NAVSSES needed were panels of the brightest people coming up with untested revolutionary ideas, and a second core of testicle hardened fund-soliciting artist.

But the way NAVSSES is structured, using Gestapo Nazi overseers that instill fear on the employees for tinkering with might be the next greatest invention. As it is presently structured, nothing of value will ever come from the place worth a second look. The WOW doesn't exist at NAVSSES because it's status quo day after day. The wait to be told verses telling what needs to be done syndrome exist throughout the organization. As long as NAVSSES creates limits on the employees' creative abilities, they will behave much like mice in a lab experiment. And like the mice, they will run the maze, as set forth by the organization for the paycheck at the end, and do nothing more. And by the way, I have never heard any of the management apologize for mistakes. Apologies go a long way towards getting people to get along and to move on.

A good manager/director, in other words, an upper management person should be the sales person of his organization. And if your talking about an organization like NAVSSES that person should be out there in the front line rubbing shoulders with the right politician, the admirals, the directors in charge of the shipyards and more. Not the sit in your office and wait for a phone call type of directors we had, including the ones that allowed the Navy shipyard to close. In the end, after the shipyard closed an audit of what the Navy receives in return for what it pays for now, when it comes to shipbuilding or repair, are a total disgrace and a big time waste of the taxpayers' monies? And don't even mention shock hardened ships, because a handful of illiterate Arabs on a rubber boat... Need I say anymore? Oh wait, so much for wasting monies on mine detecting technology too.

Our coward of a director/s job should be in the trenches talking with the people, one on one, going from department to department to inquirer about needs. Stop and smell the people and stop hiding in an office like some hideous troll breast-feeding off of NAVSEA for funding. People - what we have directing at NAVSSES, are and were nothing more than some overpaid figureheads.

NAVSSES is faltering similar to the housing loan collapse, because no one is monitoring the big wigs within the organization. Let's see, the director contact's some gnome in Washington holding the pot of gold/funding, sorry, for the purpose of carrying out some projects. The gnome reaches into his pot of funding to pay for those projects. Back at NAVSSES, the director pats himself on the back and calls the managers in for a meeting regarding the good news. Everyone at the meeting smiles upon hearing the good news, they all smile knowing that their $7000 bonuses are practically in the mail along with a letter for a job well done. The managers leave the meeting wringing their hands and report to their subordinates that their PARS (annual evaluations) are not up to par. Hey, the managers have to look like their doing a good job for getting paid all that money, plus the outrageous bonuses. A year later, all NAVSEA/Washington (the public) has to show for the funding are reams of spreadsheets a pie chart along with a heap of stinky finger pointing.

I'll say this several times throughout this book, which is a good gage of a leader's ability is to ask the people. The people I'm referring to are not the ones over them, because like crooks, they all in some form tend to do bad things. There is no honor among thieves/unmonitored managers. If there was, please explain to the public, NAVSSES, those ridiculous high pay scales the managers receive with a frosting of awards to compliment them, for what amounts for work sans any engineering or engineering oversight.

The concept of having a chain of command bossing around highly creative and talented people is stupid at best. If you want people to create the best stuff, stay out of the kitchen, just tell the cook what you want and you'll be surprised at the results.

SHIPYARD ALTERNATIVES

If the Philly shipyard was costing too much to operate, why not talk to the workers directly? Don't just close them down. Sadly, like a rotting corpse, the shipyard and anything that smells of Navy within it has been decaying ever since.

I always felt that the city of Philadelphia could have utilized the main machine shop 31 and 06 to train a lot of the inner city kids. Kids with no place to go, no training, no caring parent that in the end, these kids often ended up in prison. It wasn't like I didn't write to the city mayor or the city council. No one was listening. Believe me when I say I wrote to the City of Philadelphia; just ask any of the local newspapers how many letters they received from me, regarding just about anything and everything. The Courier Post even gave me one of their rabble-rouser T-shits. Getting back...

We had some military living quarters on the base that could have housed the city's troubled kids. The various Military Guard reserves, which in my opinion, has a slew of individuals, whose sole purpose is, once a month or whatever is to show up for roll call. And for that, these on call reservists receive a nice paycheck. Now wouldn't it make more sense to put these stand at attention reserves to work instilling discipline, teaching a trade and the list is endless, to the inner city kids? But no, it was easier to tear down the Navy living quarters buildings that were in perfect condition at the shipyard, and to sell off expensive working machinery for pennies on the thousand dollars, and or to sell the metal by weight for scrap.

By the way, the National Guard Reserves were not in battle training for war at the time. There wasn't any.

The city wasn't listening to my letters, and the Navy wasn't making rational decisions. So many of those ex-shipyard workers could have been rehired to train many of the inner city kids that often find themselves lost for employment. It's typical of many parents that have children with no thought about the child's future. The child upon graduating, if he makes it that far, is left to wander the streets asking for a job from anywhere he can.

In the end the city will pay. It will pay to keep that person on welfare, in prison or maybe none of them, if the person is fortunate enough to find a good paying job. Personally, much of the major cities inner city problems are caused by the cities ignoring the root causes, such as training the parentless children and creating jobs for them. I could speak on this subject for hours…

Thankfully, I'm here to speak up and to go after the management system from NAVSSES before anyone else is abused, harassed and worst from the present way the place is managed. We all know that absolute power corrupts, and that's exactly what is going on at NAVSSES today. And NAVSEA needs to pull their head out from their direr before asphyxiation sets in from what's going on under their watch.

What I'm trying to say before I got off track, is that the city of Philadelphia like every other city with similar unemployment needs, is for the city to provide some tangible place where a child can go to find work and training for a secure future. For me when my family arrived in New Jersey, there were only the peach fields and a handful of distant nursing homes in my area. If it wasn't for a close school friend that told me about the apprenticeship at the shipyard, there's no telling where I would be today. Just think of how many children we could keep from going to prison, if they could receive the same kind of training. And I'm not talking about the expensive technology class that rush you in and out, and at best, you graduated after building some stupid birdhouse or a couple of book ends. I talking about training in some manufacturing plant, where the student gets his hands on the heavy-duty equipment, much like a surgeon reaching in and pulling out that defective heart, and replacing it with a healthy one. The blood and gusts of machinery and the platform was there at the shipyard, only to vanish to ensure the few remaining overpaid, do zip nothing engineering engineers, would get paid high salaries.

SHIPYARD CLOSING

What occurred when the shipyard closed wasn't much different than the way irresponsible parents behave when they have children without any thought or consideration for that child's future. I know I said it earlier. No one from Washington, NAVSEA, NAVSSES or whatever crap you want to label them, had a plan that made any sense for those individuals laid-off. Many wonderful outstanding shipbuilding artisans, craftsmen and professionals were suddenly dumped to find another job. So many thinking minds were sent away, while a small handful of people decided the fate - of what, some five thousand people, maybe more? Shouldn't it have been the other way around? I'll bet a lot of those laid-off talented workers would have come up with a slew if ideas for saving the shipyard, ideas like manufacturing parts for the military aircraft, or how about making parts for the Army. And how about utilizing the dry docks for training Navy seals, or using the dry docks for scuba training, and submarine recovery research and my list can go on. In other words, the Navy needs to look beyond a handful of individuals with uniforms decked with fishing lure like bling and start talking to the movers and shakers of shipbuilding, the people themselves.

It's easy, just send out feelers, get some suggestions, analyze the results and then present it to the people. But to rely on managers and a moron of a director, come-on, these are individuals with a great retirement package and more money squirreled away in the banks that they could ever spend – why should they care one way or another of what happens to a shipyard. It's exactly why many of the huge corporate businesses fail every year. Its corporate CEOs buying and selling each others business, making huge capital gains not only for themselves but also for the scrupulous attorneys that initiate the buyouts. In the end, it's the hard working family guy that loses, a loss far greater than the upper management could ever fathom.

The shipyard wasn't being sold; it was downsized to save money. Money that eventually went into the pockets of ex-military contractors for military equipment that suddenly jumped in price, equipment like the Osprey, the

Armies Bradley crappy sinking tractor and the stealth fighter jets. Say what? You mean the stealth fighter was over priced what about all of that new technology that was put in it?

How sad to see Philadelphia go begging to a foreign country to build ships at a place where American craftsmen crafted at one time great Naval vessels. If I'm not mistaken, I Believe part of the foreign deal was to cough up forty million dollars to entice the foreigner to build ships in Philadelphia. And as expected after the builder got his money, guess what? That's right, he left as a fat cat, and the city was left to find another shipbuilder. So much expensive equipment and talent abandoned in a disgraceful mannerism, shame on the Navy and the city of Philadelphia.

WASTED SCHOOLING

So shortly after working for NAVSSES, I was asking myself, what was the purpose of wasting all that money, time and effort for those college courses, if no one in the Navy was going to give me any recognition for them? Absolutely nothing, zip, nothing - guys and girls with no college educations were being promoted which didn't make sense. I can see issuing an award for a job well done, but to promote permanently was ridiculous, especially if you compare that person against other persons who made similar efforts and performed the same kind of work. And don't tell me that the people working at NAVSSES didn't perform the same work, because we all did basically the same stuff. And if we didn't, it wasn't the person's fault; it was the supervisor favoring one person over another etc.

Sure, there were a few morons that shouldn't have been rated as engineers or even as technician, but that's where NAVSSES failed miserably. They couldn't get rid of anybody, let alone demote, someone who was deemed to be an engineer via a piece of paper, even if that person was totally void of any engineering cranium matter. You know it's true, because right now today, if I were to hand some of them a simple engineering tests, I'll bet a good number of the so called engineers working at NAVSSES would fail miserably.

Much of the failures can be traced to several factors. One is caused by years of not doing similar engineering work, and then there are those too old to remember simple calculus formulas, physics and such. No matter, because NAVSSES will still pay them as if these people were still talented as engineers should be.

THE GERMAN

To prove my point: there was one individual to relay what I'm referring to above, and that person was of German decent. He liked to sing for us during the Holidays to show off his operatic abilities. But an engineer he was not, and I tell you why. Maybe on paper he was labeled an engineer. I don't know of how many times I was called up to his cubical to show him how to do his job. The man didn't even know how to make a simple folder on his computer, and he had to write it down, as I explained and demonstrated it to him, down to the double click of the mouse. Before this so-called Navy engineer went on many of his phony ship checks, I was the one who would fill him in, on how various systems worked and what to look for.

What can I say, other than to say, that I liked the guy, but I always felt cheated for not being rated as an engineer with all my college credits, when here was a guy that barely understood high school basics? And that was after many years that we were using computers that this guy was still floundering to use his computer – go figure. I heard from many others in his group/section, who told me that this same, so called labeled engineer, was more than once escorted off a Navy ship, because he didn't know what he was doing. But time and time again, NAVSSES kept sending this phony, or maybe he was just an outdated engineer, out for ship check overtime, because no one else wanted to travel from his department. And there were other individuals just like him with similar knowledgably handicaps. Some of the foreign engineers I knew were so stupid in the engineering field; I always felt they must have been working under fake degree papers. How the heck does the Navy verify a college degree from someone claiming to be an engineer from Vietnam or one from Germany just after WWII? Especially, when the person claims to have been an engineer prior to some war in their country? Records were lost. It was easy several years ago for an engineer from India let's say; to sell a copy of his degree with social security number to another person who never attended a college. Many of them had the same name. Only now in this present day can computers check nationwide for duplications, but do they?

I know much of this because I can recall some engineers that came from Vietnam, some came from troubled parts of Africa and of course the German I wrote about. There were others and not a single one of them impressed me as being engineering savvy. I would never have allowed any of them to fix any of my appliances at home, let alone provide me with a valid calculus formula to anything. I'm for equal employment not equal stupidity.

I knew of some engineers that claimed they were paid to take the professional engineering exams for others, and there are many similar dishonest stories. The newspaper occasionally publishes a story of some big shot politician or some movie star, who received a degree either because of some huge donation or for some political agenda. And then there are the sons and daughter of politicians who received a college degree without truly attending classes and such. What is the truth, and where and when does cheating in school start and stop?

The news is full of stories where today many of the students both in school and in college cheat using the latest telecommunicating technologies. Research and term papers are bought or downloaded off the Intranet. So in the end what is NAVSSES trying to say, as it strives to gradually eliminate the hardworking technician? And then again, so what if a student in school cheated to pass a test here and there. Were they really cheating? Is it cheating to use a calculator or research some other person assembled for the world to use to the benefit of mankind? Of course the engineer didn't discover or write up the research results, but the fact that he knows where to get the information is all that matters. Isn't this what college education teaches? So what is so different between a student that spend the money and time to take a college course verses someone that knows where to get the information without having to take a specific course? Cheating? I think not, it's just a self-taught individual, who's confident in them selves.

In the local newspapers, October 3, 2008, I read where the Senate Education Committee had introduced a bill to bar educators from receiving credit from non-accredited universities. It seems that some of the higher educational degree mills were selling as many as five hundred of these phony PhD degrees per month. The bottom line for the degrees was to cash in on automatic pay raises that come with the higher education.

Here again, I say cheating? Well yes, if that's all the schools provided was a piece of paper in exchange for money and a single piece of paper. Then again, if the paper documented years of service in such field, is there anything really wrong with that person receiving the higher degree? But in my case, when I received my mechanical engineering degree from LaSalle University, Louisiana, I did do a slew of an additional ten courses to complement my college credits from three colleges in New Jersey. All I required from a reputable university like Drexel were some minor electives courses.

A person working along side a mortician, a doctor, or whatever, do they not know just as much as if that person had paid for the course, and then sat in class to hear boring lectures of material that he already understands better than the lecturer? I did some twelve years as a tool and die maker, where are my credits NAVSSES? And what about the college courses from Gloucester County College or from Camden County College or that dealt with business management and accounting? Much of what NAVSSES did was not engineer, but of business management and accounting.

If there is cheating in the educational foundations, personally it's in the major colleges and universities themselves. College presidents shouldn't be making such huge salaries for just being a figurehead. And the schools shouldn't be charging so high for so little. The other falsity colleges and Universities create is to pad on an equal amount of useless electives just to add to the cost of one of their foil stamped paper degrees.

The bottom line is that such services as health care can be drastically reduced if the Federal government would setup and run similar schools at public school fees. The market would be flooded with doctors and such. Colleges are in business to make money and at the rate they keep raising their fees this country will end up in the toilet just like the housing fiasco collapse. Colleges and Universities do not have to answer to anyone. And if you think that they do not discriminate, think again. They are institutions that cater predominately to the rich white sector of society, which can pay for such ridiculous rising costs. And this is why I say a federally funded University located in four corners of the United States is long overdue. Using public taxes to pay for someone's education to attend classes at an existing university is not the answer, since this only re-enforces the outrageous salaries many of the college CEOs presently receive. We need public universities now. By the four corners, I mean east, west, north and south, thereby making them easily accessible to the vast majority of people. No more will our students have to get their medical degrees from low cost universities such places on the Island of Grenada.

May I suggest that NAVSSES purchase a few basic copies of the Video Professor CDs, that I see advertised on television, for just about any computer subject you may want to learn about, starting with how to turn on a computer. Make sure the employees get tested after viewing those things, after-all; us taxpayers shouldn't be paying $90,000 plus salaries for incompetence. Incompetence like the German engineer or that one I met from deepest Africa or the Indian engineer I had to deal with from NAVSEA with the foggiest idea of how a knife switch operated…

PUBLIC WORKS RECOGNIZES MY WORK

Even while I was still working for Design, it took the manager from another department (Public Works) to recognize some of my excellent work. He wrote up a nice letter about how I superintended some twenty-two odd shops to construct two fire-fighting caissons for the SLEP program, the Navy carrier ships overhaul program. The caissons were an extensive project requiring calculations for floatation, and operating two 400hp water pumps to construct and make it all happen. Did my department in Design write me up for an award? Of course not, why should they? After all, I had just showed up a bunch of engineers by demonstrating that you did not require a degree to do engineering, especially the kind that the Navy required to build ships.

The Navy's phony award system isn't much different than the way Communist Russia treated their talented Russian citizens. One such example was the Russian who designed one of the first roving explorers for the Moon. The Russian big shots all took credit for the Moon landing. It wasn't until after that the person who designed the craft died was his name mentioned. Well, as you can see the Navy and other military institutes like them play this same game. It's the Navy's dirty sneaky way of giving credit to only their paper Tiger Engineers, when actually some of the best ideas are technician created and developed. Technicians have many times proven that what NAVSSES needs is not more Engineers but more technicians, the hands on people. NAVSSES does not build ships; it is in the business of fixing them up, not making new ones. Hence, NAVSSES is thinking in the idiot box. And it's the same reason why the place has way too high a salary base for products produced.

The Navy should stop keeping the expert technician doers in the shadows, and reward them more often than the already overpaid managers, supervisors and GS-13 engineers. Yeah, GS-13 engineers, these are typically engineers doing the same kind of work as all the others that are not part of management, but somehow they're making much more. Ingenuity comes from hands on experiences, and not the other way around, by hanging on to mother's skirt while daddy and mommy pays for some college vacation schooling. You know, the privileged upbringing.

JEALOUS ENGINEERS

Were the managing engineers working in Design jealous of what technicians knew and understood about the workings of a ship and more? Well, of course they were which is why technicians were rarely put in for the outstanding awards. There was no question that technicians understood all facets of building ships, since the majority of them came up the hard knots way, by building or repairing ships. Many of us understood everything there was to know about metallurgy, from welding to poured casting and more. Technicians understood all the various fasteners of hydraulics systems, to knowing the difference between a fine pitch screw and a course pitch screw fastener and everything in-between. Stress and strain calculations were child's play for us, as were everything you had to know to construct a floating combat ready ship.

Now, I'll bet you can't say that about some recent graduate right out of college holding a piece of paper with a brass colored seal. In all my thirty-nine years that I spent working for the NAVSSES, understanding calculus is not something a single engineer has had to use to repair or build a ship. No thermal dynamics, no hydraulic calculations and other high level calculations were remotely ever mentioned and for good reason. For one, the ships were already constructed, and if you had to know which hose to use or fitting to use, the working pressure and applicable fluid information was readily available imprinted on the fitting and or hose itself. If not, the information could be found in the companies catalog. So you see, it doesn't take an overpaid engineer at NAVSSES for what the Navy requires to keep it ships afloat.

And yet, from what I understand just before I retired, is that the Navy at NAVSSES is attempting to eliminate as many technicians positions as possible. In other words, they want to have a bunch of know nothings telling the Navy what it can and cannot do on ships. These are suppose to be the experts, the guys with no ship construction hands on experience. Give me a break. And I say that, because I can, you see I've known many so-called, over-rated engineers that floundered when it came to coming up with a solution of a problem on some the Navy ships. I could tell you some bungling engineering stories that could make your hairy sphincter curl up over your head, so that you would look like your wearing a cheap toupee.

ADMIRAL DIVERSITY

This email or something like it was from one of the Navy's Admiral when he emailed us regarding diversity. Basically, in it he said—"Focusing on diversity is understanding and acknowledging that each of us brings different skills, talents, knowledge, and life experiences to the fight. Obviously those things are of value to our Navy's mission, but we must look beyond that and understand that there is inherent value in the DIFFERENCES themselves. We are attempting to solve more and more complex problems with fewer and fewer people these days. We MUST maximize every possible advantage we have in order to succeed. That means tapping every resource within our reach. We simply cannot afford to overlook or exclude anyone and still hope to succeed. Thus the focus on diversity is a strategic imperative for our mission success—nothing more and certainly nothing less."

Oh really over-paid admiral, so why are the technicians being phased out, left behind, and or why are they hardly ever included in the promotional announcements and awards? What a phony letter the admiral sends us. The admiral says one thing but does something different. Children right out of college magically receive awards for what technicians consider the daily work norm. It's all a sham to get the inexperience promoted quickly. Don't believe me – try rooting through the archives of such phony awards, and you'll see for yourself. Check when the person was hired and compare that against awards. Then compare that list against senior talented employees that rarely received an outstanding award.

My proof and I got many of them, is like the young woman in my MACHALT group who was promoted shortly after I retired. She was promoted without ever having ever completed a single MACHALT project, and she never even wrote any kind of contracts for major purchase orders to solicit bids to get a project executed. She had zip knowledge of a ship's workings let alone an understanding of anyone of the hundreds of onboard ship systems. How could she receive a huge award, she just recently graduated?

That kind of disgraceful promotions that the management promotes at NAVSSES is unbelievable, downright ugly and shameful.

In the same department, a contractor doing work for us was quickly hired and promoted above the rest of us too. The fact that the contractor handled a spreadsheet of all the projects was not justification, for promoting the man, without at least allowing all the others in the group a shot at the job. A spreadsheet! Give me a break, that's secretary's work and not a GS-13 level kind of work. The management's decision to promote these two was utter stupidity, enough to drive any sane person mad. And you know what's even sadder? It's the director or the Captain blindly signing off on the promotions without investigating the fairness and the qualifications of said people. If you are supposed to be a team player (Captain/director), how is it that others in the MACHALT department were not given the same chance to compete? I say the manager was a crook for robbing the others including me, by not giving us all a fair chance to advance. If anything, the manager had to have lied about her/their qualifications to get her/them promoted.

If tragedy happens on a Navy ship and someone is killed, will NAVSSES then admit that it made a mistake from promoting the inexperienced? And what will it tell/lie to the grieving families? A folded up flag of the United States, a coffin, and a burial salute, are these the answer from mistakes from the inexperienced? Please explain NAVSSES? And God forbid, if they get off by claiming that the problems were not foreseeable, because someone used off the shelf equipment meant for non-moving systems like a house.

You see, employees that have put in the time, rarely make those kinds of mistakes because they pretty much have seen them all.

The Navy fails to understand that what makes America strong is diversity and I don't mean a kaleidoscope of colored people. Diversity comes when those individuals without a college degree are afforded the same chances to advance as those with a degree. This broadens the dimensions of freethinking. A mommy's boy is just that. He's a person raised in comfort all his life while attaining his paper pedigree that tells the world he's ready to go to work. Give me a break?

Iraqi terrorists were able to continually blowup American soldiers, because they just think differently. Why can't the military understand basic survival tactics? Managers that I have known working for the Navy at NAVSSES, seem to put in time solely fixated towards maximizing retirement and little else. The military Navy promotes with similar disregard for the elderly, the ones that put in time, experts.

I was not fodder to be ordered to rush in blindly against some machine gun nest. But that is the way I was being treated by managers at NAVSSES, with little experiences in the many factors that I described throughout this book, and others I've published.

When I was working in the Design Division of the shipyard, I picked up a ton of information regarding a slew of construction standards. It's not something you can learn in college because the subject matter was so vast and specific to every minute area of ship construction. Now don't tell me that anyone of the recently promoted children have any of that kind of knowledge and other such information. What is happening to NAVSSES is that it is becoming a very dangerous organization to use, to provide reliable advice concerning anything to do with ship construction, repair or maintenance. There are so many inexperienced working at NAVSSES that the only thing lacking at the place is a sandbox.

So here I was year after year, doing an excellent job with an impeccable leave record at NAVSSES, and guys all around me with no college, or some with just a couple of college courses under their belt were being promoted over me. How could that be? Read on...

GS RATING AND NO DEMOTION

Oh, by the way, the Government uses a pay scale that you can find on the Intranet. Ours was labeled with a GS rating, so a GS 12 grade was higher than say a GS 10 and so on. Supervisors were typically rated GS-13 and managers were GS-14. Other grade rates have been formulated since then to add to the confusion. None of the new rates makes any good sense, and it was obviously implemented to hide the fact that the secretaries can now make what an engineer does—go figure. Maybe, the new rates came about ever since women were promoted into the managerial positions. It sure seems that way to me. Laughable isn't it? And anytime one of the supervisors or managers were made to step aside for various reasons like for incompetence, you would think that the Navy would rein back their pay scale, say from a GS-13 back to a GS-12 or lower yet.

The answer is nope. So here was an ex-supervisor making the same salary, only this time, he didn't have to supervise a single person. In other words, this stepped aside supervisor was working at the level of a GS-12 engineer/technician, but he was getting paid at a hell-of-a lot more. We even had some supervisors that got so fed up with the way the place was being managed, that they requested to be relieved from having to deal with subordinates. So here they were, these ex-supervisors working all alone in a cubical while still maintaining their higher salaries. I doubt very much that such high steaks salary scenario, as I described, exists in the private industry.

The thought that there were individuals in our section making more money while doing the same amount of work as all the others — well you can imaging, the unfairness and animosity that it created. So much for being a competent director/captain.

PAY DIFFERENCES BETWEEN SHOP AND OFFICE WORKERS

What I'm about to describe relates to the way salaries were paid from when I worked as a tool and die-maker, and how it differed when I transitioned into office work. In the shop, we were under a WG rating with its typical series of pay increases steps, and that was it. When I went to work in the Design Division of the shipyard, I was placed under the GS rating system with similar step increases.

What I'm trying to get at is that in a way, no one felt cheated between one another when it came to salaries. Engineers and technicians were basically making the same, after-all; we were doing the same kind of work. To get ahead in Design, meant that you had to be promoted to one of the supervisory positions. Managers were few, so the few that existed didn't seem to matter much. So, in a way, we all kind of got along.

Then when the shipyard closed, I transferred over to NAVSSES where again, I was under the same GS pay scale system. Only this time there was a slight difference. It seemed that the longer I was there, the more I witnessed individuals around me moving ahead for what seemed like unfair promotions. And that's what they were, unfair popcorn promotions. There is no way that one person over another does any more work at NAVSSES to deserve more pay. And it is this unbalance pay roller coaster that is causing the bulk of the employees to feel unfairly treated.

Inline with promotions were the Job Descriptions, JD. JDs described what was expected between the various classes such as engineer, technician, supervisor, etc. They also were broken down according to your level of service and other such trivial parameters. Well, what the management would do was to periodically reassess the JDs to ensure that they would cover what the employee was doing or assigned projects. On the surface these changes seems justified but a closer look revealed that the changes were initiated not so much to help the lower rated technicians, as they were to help the organization save money.

What do I mean by that? It means - that if a technician were assigned a highly complex project, which are normally supposed to be handled by an engineer, the technicians JD would be altered to say that this kind of work would be expected of him in the future. By stating such complex project upgrades, the lower rated technicians in the future cannot claim or ask for a promotion, and or a special achievement award.

The way it was done was that the manager would handout copies of the JDs to the employees for review changes. Unbeknownst to the technicians, they tended to believe that by including the highly technical complex projects in their JD, that they would qualify for a promotion in the future, after-all it was all in writing, so the management couldn't deny that they did such work. Sadly those upgrades did more harm than aid the subordinates. As the years went on the technicians were expected to do more and more, while still being ignored for awards and promotions. JDs are long overdue for an honest review.

DISGRACEFUL PROMOTIONS

Let me introduce the reader to some inside information about promotions. Some of it will be obvious and some of the stuff is from my own experiences.

Does anyone dispute the fact that engineers were educated solely for that purpose of engineering? The Navy system then comes along and thinks it can make brilliant managers and accountants from them. The end results leave much to be desired. The personnel that had to deal with such moronic floundering managers often left a meeting, feeling like they had just endured a thistle stick enema session. It seems that the more repetitive meaningless paperwork you could produce, the higher up you were rated on the quarterly/semi annual performance scale. At one point, I was responding to as many as five data charts from five individuals requesting the same status for the thirty-five projects I was managing. Each one of the five individuals, a step grade over me, requested much the same redundant status information. And if they weren't, you could sense that they were being groomed for the next promotion. In other words, when you're not working or you don't have anything to do, you're asking someone else for a status report.

The stink about NAVSSES was obvious that it could make a month old cadaver covered in fresh diarrhea smell like a rose. It was like, why do we need all of these morons, all-asking for the same data? None of the same data requests arrived at the same time, so none of my information came even close to matching. And I knew it; no one gave a shit, because they never bothered to really study the charts. It was all a dog and pony show for the overpaid chiefs in NAVSEA requesting their own versions of colorful charts. And then to make it look as if they were producing something with these useless charts and bar graphs, the charts would be posted on some bulletin board like a mother might do for her child's coloring from elementary class. Some of the charts merited being exhibited in the main mezzanine/causeway of our building.

Whatever happened to posting them out on Broad Street in downtown Philadelphia, so that the taxpayers could get a look at them? Maybe one of them might find a good use for them, like using it to wrap up an oily cheese steak sandwich.

OVERPAID ADMINISTRATIVE SECRETARY

It seemed like no one understood how to transfer information from one pie chart program to another or from one data spreadsheet to another. Click and drag, cut and paste—what's that? Suddenly, because it was another crappy computer program, we all of a sudden had to learn a program that might have been upgraded; the concept of cut and paste never seemed to enter the overpaid minds, oops - I mean to say the over-paid reclassified managerial secretaries. Yes — many of the secretaries were relabeled, administrative assistant, so as to justify a huge pay raise. If you were to compare what the private sector pays such an assistant/secretary, and what the Navy pays them—you'd be shocked.

How does, a $90,000.00 salary and more sound for a phone answering assistant? Not to mentions an annual bonus awards that could add up to as much as $7000.00. And it was all for what? Answering a phone, setting up appointments, and, and, and can anybody tell me what a director's assistance does to deserve 90K plus salary? The last time I read the local newspapers in 2007, a school assistant principal was making $76,000 and the public seemed upset for paying him that much. GS pay scales whenever they come out should be published in all local newspapers, because frankly, I doubt very much that the public understands what it is getting in return. It's not like the place has engineers designing some space shuttle or even some expensive unique fiberglass sport fishing boat to justify the high salaries. Anyway back to...

And it's not like the secretaries/assistants whom were receiving such a high salaries for answering the phone, were using some of that money to dress smart or professional (not that they have too), but anyone that has seen these girls, will swear that their clothing resembles something purchased from the discount Goodwill rack hanging outdoors. And that includes the corny shoes our previous director was wearing along with his nursing home matching suit, more befitting of Michel Jackson Thriller video, for one of the dead creeps coming up from a grave.

Oh, I shouldn't say that, it's sounds too cruel. Well, it's my opinion remember, and besides, the taxpayers have to know. Actually, I've seen better clothing at the farmers market and that's after a cow has worn it.

I don't know how many times in my career as a civilian working for the Navy, that I was asked over and over again to supply the same information about myself. And yet, year after year, over paid secretaries making salaries comparable to an engineer were asking me for the same information. Frankly, I don't even know why the place had secretaries, because just about anyone of the people working there could verify, that if there was any typing to do or to schedule a travel itinerary, we all had to do our own. And that included message writing. I believe that the secretary's sole job was to handle the time keeping and to type up letters for her immediate boss. Maybe, at one time you could say that a secretary did what was typical for a secretary's work. Not any more, at least not at NAVSSES.

I suppose the title of this book should have been, The Dummying-Down of NAVSEA/NAVSSES, because it is occurring at an alarming rate from an internal paranoia about technicians - read on...

PROMOTIONS

One of the most obvious reasons for dissention at NAVSSES is due to the way individuals are being promoted. And here is a typical scenario; let's assume that you are the supervisor, with a GS-13 rate, doing the selection, from a list of qualified applicants within your department. Let's forget the fact that we all know, that the person to be promoted has already been determined. Would you "A" select the most qualified and intelligent person, or "B" would you select someone less qualified? The answer of course is "B".

So why would the less qualified applicant be selected, you might ask? Well, isn't it obvious? Why would the supervisor making the selection pick someone smarter than himself?

Isn't it obvious to the Human Resource Office (HRO) that during the next higher up promotions, that the supervisor would be competing against someone equal to or smarter than himself? But it isn't obvious to HRO. Oh no, the people I spoke to said that they don't make such mistakes, they assumed that everyone on the selection panel are honest people and that they will promote the best qualified.

Listen morons on the selection committee; leaders in the past might have hired the meanest and the badest people to be on their team for survival reasons. In an atmosphere like NAVSSES, the battle is not another foreign invading force; it's you against your fellow worker. What determines whether or not you get promoted has nothing to do with your abilities, it's if I like you. There is another factor that determines a promotion, and it says to never ever make your superiors look less than you. In other words; pretend to talk dumb when around your superiors. Say things like; "Oh, I should have thought of that, your right, I'll get right on it, I'll pay for that, I'm free – what should I do next, oh sure – when do you want to see me on the golf course, I'll try harder – where do I sign the PARS?

Listen ex-supervisors and managers, that's how dumb you presented yourselves to me.

TELL THAT TO

Yeah right, tell that to all the people from NAVSSES who had to hire an outside lawyer, to force his qualifications down the so-called management expert's throat, to show that he was qualified. Tell that to the guys that were bypassed in order to promote some unqualified secretary to a technicians position, just so that the Navy can fill a phony equal-opportunity quota. No one is opposed to filling a quota, but why promote a secretary into a technical engineering position or into a project managerial position, when there were many women on the outside that sacrificed time and effort to attend the appropriate college or technical school?

Tell that to the guy that went to college after hours in the hopes that he could qualify for a promotion. What was the sense in that person taking all those college courses if the Navy isn't going to even acknowledge his efforts? Sixty credits, or even ninety credits means nothing to the Navy, Nope you have to complete the whole slew of electives too. Electives that often have nothing to do with engineering are often what are lacking from many individuals to attain a degree.

Tell that to the elderly with years of experience over some snot-nose kid right out of college, kids without so much as a good credit score, kids that haven't even owned a home to understand financing—basically inexperienced children still living with their parents. These are kids that often can't tell the difference between Port and Starboard? They don't know Ship.

WHAT EVER HAPPENED TO EXPERIENCE?

Whatever happened to having experience? Whatever happened to giving credit for having an associate degree or x-number of credit? The Navy is supposed to set the standard for the rest of industry, instead it fails miserable. Even in many parts of the private sectors, credit is given for a two-year degree, but not in the Navy. It's all shameful behavior of the Navy and a disgrace to those who made the effort and to be told, "So what." I can't tell you of how many times that I've heard the big shot director from NAVSSES tell individuals that if they didn't like it, to quit. What an arrogant jackass, especially coming from such an overly paid buffoon with more money than he knows what to do with it. And it was a stupid thing for him to say to someone with twenty to thirty plus years of excellent service.

Shortly after I retired from NAVSSES a girl in my section recently out of college was promoted to a GS-13 position. And this was after she was promoted quickly to a GS-12 with little or no shipboard experience, certainly nothing like the experience the rest of us had. Heck, she hadn't even completed a single project and yet the $149K manager picked her for the promotion. By the way, this same manager waited until I retired before announcing the opening and another opening for a technician. How original was that? I guess the letter I sent to the captain about his demeanor had something to with it, kind of retaliation on his part I suppose. By the way, this was the same engineering girl who uploaded a meeting on the Intranet 04/07 for everyone to see, where she labeled the manager The Big Willie Cxxxxxx in the minute's memo published for our section. The Big Willie, how original, as a professional engineers is this how you address the manager? By putting him in a Big Willie did she mean Big Dick?

I write this to place a broken ammonia ampoule under the captain's nose as an alert that this guy has been retaliating ever since; I wrote the letter complaining about him. And it's the same basic reason that I decided to write this book. No hiding this in the cat litter - NAVSSES. I'm exposing the crap for all to see just how phony the place was and still is.

Man-child and girl-child is what are running NAVSSES presently; it's obvious isn't it? Children that had just about everything growing up, and these are the same children that expect high salaries after just having started to go to work, so much for having to earn your strips to a higher salary. And for the Navy to even suggest that they had to offer higher salaries to attract the new younger engineers is such B.S. And the reason I can say that is because I can prove that there is thousands of such engineers that I could recruit at a much lower paying salary. And when you consider that salaries were quickly elevated for the new comers, it becomes obvious over time that these still wet noses children will look for creative ways to make more money.

The Navy forgets that just about all of the recent recruits came on board at the lower level - so why automatically promote them when they haven't even begun to prove themselves?

The rest of us had to prove ourselves and why discriminate against those already there with years of service and talent? Don't lecture me on the word; discriminate, because the Navy has discriminated and exploited against the technician far too long? Call it what you like, but the fact remains that the Navy discriminates against people that don't have a piece of paper even though the two, the engineers and the technicians, do exactly the same work. As a matter of fact, the technicians in most cases were more adapted to better resolving shipboard clichés than a paper-trained person.

What ever happened to equal pay for equal work according to the Navy's ethics working contract to the people?

And to all the supervisors and managers that might have felt that I was a threat to your advancement, or were scared of how much I could have made you look so stupid at meetings, I say this, "You can now remove that long-lasting barbed enema stick out of your exit orifice that kept you talking and acting nasty while I was there." Hopefully, the other subordinates will have it a bit easier while you heal.

Recently in the local newspapers, I read a study that was done on college student grades and competency. And it wasn't news to me that what they found was that a large majority of students were cheating at every turn. Sadly the colleges didn't really care and seemed to be more concerned with turning out the number of graduates. More graduating meant more money for the school and so on.

And there was another article in the local papers April 25, 2008, about West Virginia University awarding Governor Joe Manchin's daughter, Heather Bresch, a master's degree when she did not earn one. This is a classic case where a University was caught cheating, and it was caught ONLY because it involved an important political person. I've mentioned others and I'll mention degree cheats to follow.

I don't know, but if I were in charge of hiring new recruits just out of college for my money, I would have them prove their abilities by taking a test based on their major. But not at NAVSSES, if you have a degree your hired, "Welcome aboard. Anything you say has to be right by us."

NAVSSES is not Iraq or Afghanistan where these new recruits are working under severe conditions and under the threat of death everyday. NAVSSES is luxury working conditions sprinkled with a huge dose of boredom, so much so, that many have taken to opening up their own convince stores to keep busy. Candy, sodas, pretzels anyone? See some of the pictures at my website at larryandjane.com.

THE SHEET METAL WORKER

And if you don't believe that supervisors select the less experienced, here is my experience for a similar promotion when one of the supervisors in our Machinery Alteration Department (MACHALT) was on the selection panel.

I applied for a supervisory position when it was advertised. Only to be told via a letter from personnel department that I didn't even qualify. So I challenged their reasoning. I asked them; how come some guy with no college background, with just a sheet metal working background qualifies for the supervisor position interview, while someone like me with a degree in accounting, a degree in management and an associate in Mechanical Engineering doesn't qualify? That's three separate degrees, plus a business running several rental properties.

They didn't know how to respond except to take back my application and grant me an interview. I suppose that they were not expecting anyone to challenge them. The they, I'm referring to were from the personnel office. I suppose the person had marching orders, and it was obvious that my section manager already knew whom he wanted for the promotion.

The brick and mortar was already set in stone—my application wasn't going to change anything. They were going to allow me to be interviewed with a bunch of ear-plugged interviewers. One of our department's supervisors, Rotty, was one of the interviewers. An ex-secretary himself when he first came to work at NAVSSES, with just a couple of basic college courses under his belt, against mine with multitude of managerial to high level engineering courses, and what chance did I have that he would select me? Nope, instead an ex-sheet metal worker was selected; a person who struggled to use his computer, and this was when computers were in their simplest form.

When the Navy first began issuing computers to all of the office personnel, the newly promoted so-called ex-sheet metal supervisor, fought against having to use one. He would deliberately pound his fist on the keyboard in frustration. "This is a secretary's job, I shouldn't have to be typing anything," he would say as he floundered to grasp its functionality. I just hated to hear him pound on the keys like the gorilla in the suitcase commercial. It was obvious that computers were too much for this guy to comprehend.

At the time, I had already written a couple of technical manuals, designed a solid state fueling system for aircraft carriers, and I handled just about all the alterations in our group that dealt with complex hydraulic governor system or electrical equipment. Plus, I had experience managing at a movie theatre and several rental properties, not to mention half dozen patents. So anyway, here I was with this excellent mechanical and electrical experience, with an excellent leave record, a slew of college courses, and I could speak a couple of foreign languages, I traveled the world and understood different classes of people and races. I always had no problem making the impossible possible. There was so much more to list it all here, and yet the Navy decides to pick a South Philly boy, one who only understood how to hammer sheet metal and rivet it together. Where was his experience?

And the Navy thinks that they picked this guy, because he was smart or experienced—Wow! The gorilla on the keyboard retired almost immediately after our laptops appeared on the scene. I wonder why?

If anyone required supervision it was the sheet metal worker, not me. There isn't a single supervisor or manager from the shipyard, or from NAVSSES who can ever claim, that they had to help me with any of my assignments. I could run with any of them no matter the complexity. I would have made a great leader and motivator, as anyone knows that has spent some time with me. There wasn't a subject I wasn't in tune with from wildlife to the most complex digital electrical circuits and more… There's one thing I never had to say, and that is what I heard said from the female director, when she indicated she knew nothing about her new position. Oh yes, an inexperienced suckling.

The ex-sheet metal worker grew up and spent his whole life in Philly. What does he know about people in general and other cultures? It was obvious Rotty, one of our supervisors, had already picked who he wanted for the promotion. I had a much more knowledgeable background from operating heavy equipment, a background in tool and die making trade, I rebuilt many homes, I ran a farm, I rebuilt many cars to the utmost degree, I wrote my own patents, I served years in various design divisions, and I had much more social experiences from traveling and living in different parts of the world. Plus, I knew two other foreign languages and I had; now get this, over one hundred credits in College at the time. Go figure, can you believe it? Here was a guy with very limited abilities selected to supervise people like me.

So what if you knew other languages, you might ask. Well, for one it was one of the questions on the application, therefore it must have meant something. Plus there's no question that someone that understands different cultures is more in tune with dealing with diversity in people. Verses someone that lived his whole life in one particular city like Philadelphia, where hoagies, cheese steaks, and the possibility of partaking in the annual Mummer's parade as a clown is a given.

Since I said something earlier about the selection supervisor, Rotty, for a promotion, I might as well mention just how rude he was as a supervisor in our department that I found offensive. I mentioned that the tin sheet metal worker was promoted basically to ensure that when Rotty applied from his GS-13 position to a higher paying GS-14 position, Rotty would ensure that he was a shoe-in to get it. Maybe, the metal worker was picked for the promotion because like his boss, he too grew up in Philly. The supervisor, Rotty, graduated from an art school, Oh wow. Don't ask me how he got promoted to a technical supervisory position with a background in art, but he was promoted all the way up to a GS-14 position in the Platform office when he finally retired in 2007.

So why should Rotty select me to be his equal as another supervisor at his GS-13 level? I was a GS-12 at the time, and a promotion would have meant that I was his equal. I'll tell you why. Like I pointed out earlier and I'll keep repeating it, that the supervisor making the selection was afraid that if I was promoted, he would have to compete against me for the next higher up GS-14 managerial position. Rotty knew that he would not stand a chance against all my college background and past experiences. This supervisor once admitted to a bunch of us in the office that when he came to work for the Navy, he worked as a secretary, and that over time he was promoted to a supervisory position. But that wasn't what he put down on his resumes–I have a copy of his qualifications and it did not say secretary, maybe, he started at a GS-3 level.

For the ex-secretary supervisor, it made more sense to compete against a sheet metal worker than against someone like me with all my background abilities. And this was one of the reasons why I was against such promotional practices that are considered illegal in the private sector. The Navy's promotion system rewards the less talented, the dummying down system.

Does it make sense to have a person who lived his whole life in one city as your spokesman to communicate with a space alien, or would it make more sense to use the person that traveled the universe? It's the same reason the CIA and FBI failed miserable in understanding the Arabs way of thinking until it was too late. Bin Ladin got away because of some idiot in Washington with a piece of paper, remember. It's the same losers at the FBI and CIA that weren't talking with one another, and it's the same commanders from all the military sources that suddenly found themselves in difficulty communicating between the forces during the Iraq War.

And how was it that the Pakistani father of the Atomic Bomb, Khan was able to sell his plans to North Korea – CIA must have been asleep, drunk or chasing whores overseas? If we had to account for every dollar at NAVSSES, why is the CIA allowed to spend with just the opposite accounting, especially after seeing how easily the desert dwellers got away with what they did, time and time again. An embassy, a Navy ship, the twin towers parking garage and then taking down two towers, the Pentagon and passenger plane out west. Am I wrong? By the way, for them to blame their failure on antiquated equipment, and the lack of communications between organizations, that is such bunk. The fault of the attacks was and still is an elitist boneheaded mentality. In other words under government run organizations, I got my promotion so I'm smarter than you.

Please explain the story about Ali A. Mohamed, a radical ex-Egyptian Army officer who toyed with the intelligence services while joining our Army? This guy was part of the 9/11 attacks thanks to our paper tigers, the Army's brainiac security system. It's time for the Navy like the Army's bungling to stop bobbing for logs in the porcelain bowl as they seek answers to new underwater technology and come up for a breath of fresh air ideas.

Not to get off track regarding communicating, but here are some mannerisms about Rotty, our supervisor, when he was in charge in my section.

Around the office, one of Rotty's bad habits was to walk around in the morning to tell us all about his personal stuff that went on about his new home in South Jersey. He would describe its pool in minute detail, etc. Or he would tell us about a movie he saw over the weekend down to the littlest details. It was all, boring, but we all pretended to listen. Finally, when he was all done speaking, Rotty would follow-up his standup BS with, "So what did you do this weekend?" As I started to tell him about something I did, or movie I saw over the weekend, he would look away for another fellow worker and totally ignore me in the middle of my conversation.

This supervisor wasn't interested in anything I had to say; he just wanted everyone else to hear his crappy home stories. Rotty's office mannerisms were always rude. And it wasn't with just this supervisor; I noticed this same rudeness was common amongst other managers and even some of the captains. If you weren't at their level or higher rated, you might as well consider yourself fodder. You were just another rung of a rickety bridge stung over a torrential river below deep in some jungle in Brazil, where your every word is muffled by the sound of rushing water. No one cares about the people at NAVSEA/NAVSSES; it's every person for himself. The higher one is in the rung the deeper a subordinates voice becomes to the depth of the river.

And I can say that because if anyone cared they would have saw to it, that I received credit for my efforts or even mention what I had to do to get the Engineering label. Nope, not even a label change was I entitled to even if it meant that I still maintained the same GS-12 rate. It just goes to show you, that all my supervisors and managers were jealous and basically two-face.

My questionable ex-supervisor, Rotty, that selected the metal worker to become a supervisor instead of me, was eventually promoted up another step, when he moved from our section to the Naval messaging center or as it's called, the Platform office. There, he eventually got a GS-14 promotion. I quickly learned to stay away from the jerk after he maliciously forwarded one of my simple joke Emails, to my manager. I thought he would have appreciated the simple cartoon. Why was he trying to get me in trouble? I found out about his back stabbing from my present supervisor. He was one of the many in the line supervisors who replaced Rotty.

What did I ever do to that moron for him to be such a Big Ass Hole? I'll never know. I did send him an email that just said "Thanks." In other words you're a Big Dick.

I was glad to see Rotty finally retire in 2006. Unfortunately, he was hired by one of the major contractors the Navy uses. His promotions never made any sense at all, because the jerk never ever responded once to any of my request for information or for funding for any of my projects, when he was working in the amphibian section of the platform office. I even complained to my bosses about him ignoring my messages, but no one was listening or maybe they were lacking testicles to speak up for me. I suppose you could say that this all happened, before the two-face, Rotty, was into his backstabbing. I just learned to go around him if I had to get something done from the amphibian platform section. And yet, the Navy found Rotty competent enough to promote him up and up.

When he was a GS-12 as a supervisor in our section, Rotty would change into a bathrobe with matching slippers. And to complete his Hue Hefner look, he smoked a pipe. That was Rotty per my opinion, another office clown promoted as a competent professional, just what the Navy wanted. From what I knew him and his abilities, the two-face was a failure. Rotty was pretty much like the so-called paper tiger engineers, in that he would tell you all about his home projects in boring details.

In other words, when you're an artist, like myself, a painting isn't a big deal; you can easily knock out another painting. When you're a klutz - you tend to tell everyone about your achievements in detail. But to the people that knew Rotty in the platform office, he was very much liked. I suppose when your at the top of your working scale and made it without much substance—how could you come to work with an upsetting agenda, a sad personality or whatever? People have to like you - no one likes a complainer.

I happen to see retired Rotty when I was shopping at Lowey's one day in 2008. I could see that he recognized me, but I made no move to say, Hi, least I give him any satisfaction for his evil mannerisms, as a boss, when we worked in the same MACHALT (Machinery Alterations) department. I suppose when you can't enjoy the company of an ex-co-worker, it's got to feel like a punch in the gut.

WASTED MY TIME

A promotion like the limited experienced sheet metal bender proved my worst fears. All my college courses were a waste of my time and money. Taking the courses after work, night after night, for years didn't matter. The Navy's so-so managers were promoting whom they wanted, and it had nothing to do with that person's ability to perform at the higher level. Many of these so-called supervisors if you ask me had the mental ability of a janitor, with a mop in one hand and a toilet plunger in the other. These were the guys that were selected for their important decision making abilities—lead the charge with a plunger sort of speak. If any of them were better than that, show me. Show me what was so great about him, his team playing abilities, his creations, discoveries – no, none – I thought so. Please don't show me another useless toilet paper chart. Show me something tangible.

Take note, that I wasn't the only one who felt betrayed by the Navy. There were others whom made sacrifices and struggled to better themselves only to be abandoned and insulted for their efforts.

Don't get me wrong. I'm not out to make enemies out of my co-workers; many of them were great guys. But when it came to promoting the most qualified—the Navy fails miserably by using draconian methods presently exercised. Even the Union proved on numerous times, that NAVSSES managers cheated to promote whom they like, not who was more qualified. Highly qualified employees should not be

OTHER EXAMPLES

Here are some other macabre examples of the disgraceful ways the Navy often promoted stupidity; one reason often given by the Navy; was the student is just out of college, so he must be smarter. Or they might say something like; we need new blood with fresh ideas. That statement made as much sense as having fresh mud for brains—the students just out of college in almost all cases were never married, they never owned a home, they never paid serious bills, they never built a home, they never ran a company or started one and much less other achievements, and yet some idiot in the Navy's management system felt that these wet nosed kids just out of diapers were more qualified as supervisors and managers.

You can imagine how big the kids' heads got to; knowing that they were being promoted over others much older and with much more experience. And yes, the Navy is heavily delinquent in discriminating against the elderly, I happen to be one of them. The girl that was promoted almost to the day after I retired is a prime example of discrimination against the elderly, and that same promotion demonstrates discrimination against those in my office that still remained working. These kids were nurtured all the while that they attended college with all expenses paid, so where is their independent thinking, the creativity? I know what it is? It's that piece of paper with a foil seal, how appropriate is that? A piece of paper that in some so-called universities is often bought instead of honestly earned.

And don't lecture me about the benefits of a degree because at NAVSSES, none is truly required, especially when only less than 1% of the work has anything to with engineering. And for that less than 1%, all the calculations have already been done, and they are available from the original manufacturer of the product.

Hiring recent college graduates is like ordering koi by the fishnet scoop from a pet store. There is no telling what your prize fish will look like, as they get bigger. Some will look gorgeous worthy of prizes and others will look bland with defects. But they're your fish, you've raised them and now you feel guilty releasing any of the defects to some river nearby or flushing them. And that is the way NAVSSES does business when it hires new recruits and then fails to cull away the fluff.

Back to… I arrived at that figure of less than one percent, by roughly estimating that if five people are truly doing engineering work and dividing that by the number of employees, some 1500. That comes to less than one percent. But in reality, something like two people have a project that might be considered of engineer caliber, so now the percentage is one half of one percent. Is anyone awake at NAVSEA or Carderock to notice that something has to be done about the waste fraud and abuse? Stop the arrogance and denial now – Department of Defense Pentagon Navy.

And what about being married? Ok, some of you might argue that marriage is not an issue when determining whether a person can be promoted to a supervisory position.

My answer to that is that it doesn't have to be marriage. Sometimes couples that have lived together certainly understand cohabitation/getting-along, arguing and dealing with others etc., certainly much better than boys or girls whom have lived their whole life under parental nurturing. Many of the recent graduates are just coming off of an allowance while they were in still in school, and the Navy turns around and right off the bat, places these same kids in charge of huge projects, carte blanc accounting and in charge of veterans, experienced engineers and technicians. That kind of management thinking is about as bright as a proctologist using a catcher's mitt in place of a rubber glove.

Just wonderful, and the Post Office cannot understand why they have a problem with suicides and in-house shoot-outs. Would anyone of you reading this ever hire an inexperience homebuilder to construct your home? I think not. So why is the Navy promoting the inexperienced. Those, how you say, those people that are in the dark, which haven't moved into the gray to eventually become light. HELLO NAVY – WAKEUP! These young minds are still in the dark where parents have led they way with a candle of decision making. No wonder INSURVS reveal incompetence that originates from NAVSSES and trickles down to the ship's force. For those unfamiliar the INSURVS, they are periodic ship service inspections to make sure a ship's equipment operates properly.

And NAVSSES personnel please don't even mention, that I wouldn't have qualified because the announcement was for an engineer. Engineer my ass; there is nothing, absolutely nothing that we did in the MACHALT or any other department at NAVSSES that required an engineer for anything what so ever. The person who proposed that announcement opening couldn't name a single area in the MACHALT program, that requires an engineer to run it, and that includes any of the managers' position. As a matter of fact, we had a technician who originally created the MACHALT department as proof. And that ex-technician did a far better outstanding job than any engineer manager at NAVSSES could ever hope to achieve.

The proof is that that same technician was promoted all the way up to a GS-15 position. So there you go, I can prove over and over again in just about ever department that NAVSSES and NAVSEA have been deliberately discriminating against technicians. It's oblivious, that the existing NAVSSES cost of doing business is skyrocketing, due to a distorted director's view that NAVSSES requires more engineers than technicians, engineers which cost more for less or similar output. Is this what NAVSSES calls doing good business, getting things done, moving ahead, cost cutting, the future…

Give me a break. What ever happened to earning your strips/promotions via multiple years of experience instead? No wonder it's costing the Navy so much to get anything done. The navy is way overpaying for inexperience – Wake up society and demand your government do something besides producing pie charts.

The Navy's selection of children right out of college is like a mental anchor, which is hard to break. In other words, the Navy has dropped a mental anchor in believing that children right out of college have much more intelligence with nothing to back it up to prove it, other than a piece of paper. The proof is in how the pay scales have risen at a ridiculous runaway rate for so little in return. There should be a scale much like some of the schoolteachers have to undergo to prove teaching results. As it presently stands, the Navy has no such scale. It's time for the Navy to pick up that anchor and set a new coastline. The ships are presently marooned in a bureaucracy of do nothing managers at NAVSSES, managers which find creative ways of padding on more money via outrageous awards and phony overtime reporting.

Intelligence is a vast subject and it does not reside on a bleached document with fancy lettering on it made from pressed wood pulp. I'll admit that it's gauge to measure against for starters, but that's it. What do you call a guy like Bill Gates, the Chairman billionaire of Microsoft? He never graduated with a college degree. Or how about the space pioneer Burt Ruttan? Here was a guy that on his own with just a handful of friends has done all kinds of first of its kind, from inner orbital space flights, to flying around the world in his own specially designed aircrafts.

I know it sounds a bit off when I mention people like Gates, but not really because it's all related. At NAVSSES there were talented people, but the place kept them pinned up like tasty cookies in a fancy tin box. NAVSSES deflates those individuals that create outside the box by gradually handing them lower and lower performance evaluations. Bill Gates had parents that understood that their son had a dream and they supported him. It was the same with Butt Ruttan.

At NAVSSES the talent is there, but like the cookies in the tin, over time, they become stale. Creativity for these people atrophies, and what's left? Sports scores, maximizing retirement benefits and phony awards for a select few are what are left.

So while some of us have city street smarts, some have outdoors smarts and there are those into the numbers world from investors to those immersed into some form of science. A college degree is not a requirement in any of these fields, anymore than it was required at NAVSSES. For example, I learned more on my own such as computer programming, chemistry, solid-state electronic circuitry, robotics and I could go on, without any schooling from attending college on the subjects. Even, when I was taking college courses at Camden County or at Drexel, I would spend hours studying in the library, especially when something didn't make sense from the way the professor was teaching it. Or I would just spent the time in the library to learn some subject on my own, because I enjoyed learning about anything and everything. So while a huge chunk of the engineers and technicians whom I knew at NAVSSES, were into spending hours studying games involving a ball of some form, I spent my time on constructive studies. I'm not insinuating that all of them did so, only that just about all whom I knew did so.

Oops, I have to say engineering friends like Nick, Ted and Jim were some of the few who went off to indulge into engineering projects at home. But at the office there was nothing that could be considered engineering, which a technician could not resolve. So while some of my co-workers might think it was engineering to give them selves a big head, it really wasn't if you want to compare it with some of the work that comes out of companies like Motorola or Martin.

Intelligence might be gray to some, but if I were hiring engineers to build my ships, I wouldn't be picking up the guys that memorized last month's baseball score. But then again, NAVSSES doesn't build ships; it's just a conduit to the shipyards and or the contractors that did and does build them.

NAVSSES did have some programs, not privy to the technicians, where the engineers were to read some material and then take a test at the end, kind of an engineering refresher thing. If you were anything less than an engineer, NAVSSES would consider you too dumb to take the high school level refresher. Just another one of those things NAVSSES does to keep all others not papered down.

Sounds a bit like repressing Blacks and Women to me. They too dumb to advance, boogie, boogie - Stupid Jackass Bottom Feeding Management System in my opinion.

NO ACCOUNTING EXPERIENCE

Here is another dirty secret that the Navy managers play to keep someone from being promoted. They keep specific personnel from seeing all funding documents, or they prevent that person from receiving any training related to funding, that way they can tell the person that he doesn't have any accounting experience. But ah, what about my accounting degree or my business management degree? Don't they count for something? You mean to tell me, that all my past experiences building homes, owning and operating heavy construction equipment, owning and running seven rental homes plus running a computer business from home doesn't count too? And what about my excellent credit report, verses some kid just out of college or even the sheet metal workers credit report? Why doesn't the Navy use someone's credit report as one of the factors in determining promotional qualifications? I know mine was fantastic, I can't say the same for some of the young people.

Again, would anyone of you place a child in charge of your retirement investments? And yet, NAVSEA and NAVSSES do just that with millions of taxpayer dollars.

Frankly, if you know how to balance a checkbook, knowing how to manipulate a job order is Child's play. Get Real idiots at NAVSSES. Oh, and by the way, that was a top management decision to keep the technicians away from handling job orders and such. That must have taken a lot of gray matter creativity to come up with that decision. There's no question that the majority of the engineers at NAVSSES have never seen, or prepared, a cash-flow statement, or seen a profit and loss statement. I was straight "A" in College accounting. I have an accounting certificate, but NAVSSES denied me a chance at a promotion by stipulating that I never handled any of the funding, which was deliberately kept away from me.

Job orders were and still are often handled by some secretary with a high school education promoted to some new position, with the word accountant in the title somewhere. But Technicians, Oh my God forbid, if they were allowed to handle job orders. This is nothing more than the evil directors forcing technicians in a box thereby stifling their thought processes.

DICTATING WHO GETS WHAT

And here is another nasty dirty trick that the Navy uses to keep certain people down or prevent them from getting promoted. They do it by dictating who gets what project. Some individuals seem to always get the easy jobs and others receive the more complex stuff. Guess which one gets promoted. Your right - it's the guy that does the least amount of work. And why is that? It's done because the more knowledgeable person is needed in the field working on the ships, where his expertise can be best utilized, so much for knowing your job. A supervisor on the other hand, just needs to keep feeding his subordinates more work, make sure his people aren't leaving the premise five minutes early, and making other such trivial aboriginal Bedouin decisions.

Face it—others like me were considered a threat, to what amounts to a nursing home of creative ideas. When a person is experienced or an expert in a particular piece of naval equipment, his chances of getting promoted tend to vanish. And there's a reason for why the Navy does this. For one, why would you send someone to troubleshoot a problem on a ship that is inexperienced? So hence, the less-skilled individuals get promoted at levels where all they have to do is issue orders and assign specific tasks. A layoff for these do nothing people is out of the question. And to think-they get paid a lot more.

While I'm on the laid-off subject, I should mention this nasty trick that was tried by one of the managers to get rid of one of the secretaries that he didn't like. It went something like this; the questionable secretary got sick and took sick leave. When her time was up to return to work she contacted her supervisor about returning. The supervisor during the conversation assured the secretary that it was ok to stay out an additional couple of days. Meanwhile, unbeknownst to the secretary, another new attractive hire was placed in her position.

The original secretary suspecting something was wrong contacted one of her Union representatives. The rep informed her that unless she had it in writing that she could stay out the two additional days, she wouldn't have a leg to stand on. She could be fired. The secretary returned immediately to the surprise of the new hire... In other words the not so liked original secretary was being set up. I won't mention who told me this story but...

NEED ENGINEERS WITH
A PASSION

For an engineer that truly understands engineering, that person needs to be someone that has a passion for the business. Often times, this is not the case at NAVSSES. It's kids taking engineering courses solely for the monetary awards, or they were children corralled into that major because it was what their parents wanted. I don't know how many of the so-called engineers that I met at NAVSEA and NAVSSES that had no clue about the basics of how their automobile operated, or even how a simple light switch on the wall operated. I kid you not. I had one engineer, come in Monday morning and go into his long story as if he were wiring up the space shuttle, as he explained how he changed out the light switch in his living room. I had to hear all nuances of how he inserted his screwdriver, and how it all made sense to him after looking inside the switch box. That's what NAVSSES labels an engineer in most cases.

Not to brag but I was one of the few that many people could come to for a problem about their car or anything to do with nature. I must have answered some 6000 on line requests regarding car problems, until I gave it up because it was hurting many of the auto mechanics. When it came to understanding automobiles, there were many at work that knew that I had engine parts lying around my office space just for show and tell. I not only understood how all the individual components interacted, I knew how they were put together. That is a mechanical engineer.

There was another individual that worked for NAVSEA in Washington. This guy was of Indian decent from India, not that it should matter, but what I was getting at was that this supposed engineer could not comprehend a simple knife switch, when I presented one to him from one of the ships. I had to describe how it operated as if I was talking to a school child. Shoot – I was building transistor radios at nine years old and transmitting voice on radio at thirteen and much, much more - see my other books. NAVSEA did us all a good service by laying-off some 50% of their workforce. Thank God for that, because the Indian kept bugging me for status reports so that he could look good at his job, a freeloader you might say.

RUDE MANAGER

Let's see, if you fit this description-you silly Ms. manager? Some bitchy person once mentioned something about a technician who was promoted from working in the shop as a supervisor to working for NAVSSES in an office job. This individual was an excellent worker and remained at a technician GS-12 level for many years. So when a friend mentioned it to the Ms. manager that this guy was long over due for a promotion, you're not going to believe what the Ms. manager making roughly $149K, a GS-14 said. She said, "He should be lucky that he's still not working in the shop."

By the way, the person who said that was lucky to have been promoted to the position that she was, because frankly, I know for a fact that she couldn't and she did not complete a single one of her projects in the MACHALT program, when she was quickly promoted to a GS-12 level and upward to her GS-14 position. Ok, we all know, that many of the women at NAVSSES were quickly promoted over the men, with a ton of experiences, to fill nothing more than marching quota orders from Washington D.C. God forbid, if it were orders to fill some heart surgeons positions. How many of us would want one of these ladies to do the transplant.

So back to… The hard working tech retired and was quickly hired by a major Navy contactor to manage the business. Go figure? The contractor understood what they had, not the Navy. Oh no, and the reason is because of the snot-nose overly promoted engineers at NAVSSES are, face it, JEALOUS! The outstanding technician left with that invisible Navy infantry's bayonet in his chest. How sad is that?

I forgot to mention that the bitchy manager got her promotions under the upward mobility for women, and it had nothing to do with her having experience. Her inexperience shows itself when she speaks.

ROTATING SUPERVISORS AND MANAGERS

And here is yet another ugly way that the Navy wrecks your chances of being promoted, the Navy rotates the supervisors and mangers. On the surface, it all sounds legit and beneficial for the management, and in a way, I suppose you could say it does help them, but only them. The very fact that my supervisor was moved to another department does just the opposite to those lower rated people left behind. With each new manager, and I had a crap load of them, I had to retrain them about my abilities. You have no idea of how hard that could be, especially, if the new supervisor came into your section with an agenda. Things like a new recruit right out of college might look promising to the new supervisor, and hence the new student with zip experiences receives all the attention followed by a quick promotion. "Here, let me show you around, I'm the new sheriff around here, so anything I say or do is ok. Care to take a trip to wherever with all expenses paid? How about if I let you put together a spreadsheet of all the projects my people are working on, and if you do a good job, I'll see to it that you get promoted. Here kiss my hand."

That people is the mentality of what I witnessed going on a NAVSSES. What new recruit is going to argue with that? The recently hired are often so humbled to be hired that we know that they tend to behave like puppy dogs with that innocent look about them. You know we all do it and the people in charge are no different. It's that new friend or baby smell that get the best of us to spill our guts. The only thing missing at NAVSSES is a Catholic priest to take confession, because frankly, the place is exploding with need to tell stories. OK, maybe not a priest (molestation wink, wink). A psychologist might be more appropriate.

The girl that received the promotion immediately after I left the place was one of these students, and the supervisor/manager was himself, new to our section. His mistake was in assuming that I was a pushover until I pretty much put him in his place with my letter to the captain, spelling out the way he can and cannot talk to his people. My ex-supervisor/manager was so frustrated from my letter that he did try a couple of times to retaliate. In one of his insults he tried to belittle me by insulting one of my spreadsheets that listed our entire up and coming prototype installations. I had lots of information on the spreadsheet about each project, but to this supervisor/manager, he criticized it via an Email that said my remarks on the spreadsheet were so seventh grade. So much for abbreviating verbiage to say something, especially in areas of my spreadsheet with limited space. A month later, we received an Email from him that indicated that we no longer had to submit an updated spreadsheet, which we had to do every week along with a status report that I know no one ever read. Much of it was just busy or duplication of work, because the field reps had already forwarded the progress of project installations.

Managing a new group of people can be a daunting experience and it helps if the new leader takes the time to get to know his people, verses trying to find faults in them. People will be on guard much like we all do when friends stop over to visit at one's residence. If you push them, they will push back and some may even sabotage the end product.

Pushing back can take on an assortment of subtle forms from waiting to be told what to do next, to avoiding jobs by pretending to have ill family members and so on. Some of the employees would pretend to be at the test sites (another building some four blocks) just to kill time. And there were those that volunteered for all the traveling so that they could spend time at some remote nightclub bar or whatever visiting friends.

So when our section received a new manager with a history of insulting subordinates and an attitude, it was inevitable that there was going to be some clashes of personalities. Hence, my letter to the Captain to rein him in before things worsened. Our new manager was basically a bully, rather than try to understand what we were about; he pulled out a weapon (document subtle misunderstandings) and proceeded to threaten us via our annual evaluations. Big mistake...

Our new manager's initial priority should have been to be a team player and not a faultfinder. By that I mean that when he came in to our section, he went through our status reports and spread sheets with a fine toothcomb looking for any discrepancies. He had everyone pointing fingers at one another by demanding that he be included on all inter office emails. And he specifically indicated in one of his emails that all mistakes would be documented and used to rate our annual evaluations. The manager's credibility is in the toilet when using such questionable sinister behaviors. That's like the little sneaky kid telling you that he is going tattle on you for whatever. "I'm going to tell Mommy." Talk about a comfortable person to work under…

What ever happen to understanding that all of us make mistakes, or we need time to know what your new agenda is all about?

The fact that one of us failed to look at one of two-dozen spreadsheets during a week period is asinine, and it was no reason to write up the person. But this idiot of a manager was doing just that. Ghee, if you want to look at this spreadsheet verses this other one, ok, now I know… please don't beat me? Suddenly when this moron of a manager came on the scene, the anxiety of everybody in my section went sky high, except for the cutesy recently hired engineer that was rushed through promotions, as was a newly hired ex-contractor. Yeah right, two recent hires with little knowledge about our program and they received accolades, awards and much more money to boot, go figure.

This particular manager had an air about him that he could do it all, and that he had all the answers, instead of relying on his workers, to help him make his work flow smoothly with quality results, and under budget. No one disputes that a leader's job is to take charge and make things work. Humiliating employees isn't the way and neither is using headstrong tack-ticks, especially when dealing with similar or higher intelligent and experienced people.

Another mistake this manager made was to set a clear agenda for just two people. If anything, his agenda was targeted against just two individuals verses three other individuals in the group. I was one of them and one other person, we were the only two to receive a signed insulting like letter of what he expected from us. The letter was so ridiculous, that I taped it up in my office booth for the duration of my stay. That letter was part of my complaint to the Captain by the way. I had been in the MACHALT department since its inception some eighteen years ago. I did not need some outsider suddenly telling me that he expected this and that he expected that and blah, blah, blah from me.

Why weren't the others given such a letter? My annual ratings were always highly sat even though I always felt I should have been rated outstanding. I never fell behind in any of my projects, and for a long time I was handling as many as thirty-six projects. When the new sheriff appeared, I believe I was down to just five projects, and many of them had zip funding. So what was his beef, I'll never know other than that he was acting like a bully. Someone mentioned that he had not been picked for a promotion, which may have accounted for his ill-timed actions when he was put in charge of our section.

STATUS REPORTS

Ah yes, that status reports which no one ever read because they were so boring. Much of it was the same information coming in from the various departments and coming from the field representatives. I know I just said it, but I'm writing it again since I'm mainly writing for the Navy. There was so much useless information that no one could get his head around any of it. Maybe, if the status reports were divided per specific ship affected, there might have been some order in them to where anyone could understand them. But as it was, each department submitted a report each week of basically what that individual was doing. Much of the reports were faked just to make it appear as if the person was submitting something. And there was a good reason for submitting something even if was garbage, you see supervisors, like the one I had indicated that he was keeping a tally of how many status reports we submitted, a tally that could affect our semi-annual evaluation. Get a low scale, and he can deny you a bonus thereby ensuring that he in turn receives a big bonus all to himself. In other words, he's taking your share of the block funded award money pie.

So while some individuals got away with rarely submitting status reports, others were being tortured to come up with something or risk having their semi-annual evaluation down graded. It was just another tool that some supervisors used as a method to retaliate against an individual, whenever he wanted. And trust me, there were masochists that took pleasure on insulting subordinates amongst them. And if think that the Navy would do anything to these misbehaving, power tripping managers, you would shocked to know that the Navy does it's best to protect them. So, while a lower rated GS 11 or lower person might be dismissed for an infraction, anyone at the management positional scale is protected in a cloud of do no wrong secrecy. Management protects their own colleagues no matter how harmful and corrupt they are. That sinister management cloud is there to protect the Navy from being sued; after all if one of the managers gets demoted or dismissed, the Navy understands that the person harmed can retaliate with a lawsuit.

Which is why, you will rarely see anyone in the management get relieved from the work place. Instead, what you'll see happening, about a questionable manager and or supervisor, is that they will be moved to another department if enough people in his section complain about him, or NAVSSES management will try to move the person who filed the complaint to another department.

The ugly part about not demoting the trouble-causing manager is that, when the Navy does not do that, they are playing with fire, the kind that can at times get someone killed. Insults hurt more than a punch in the face, but the Navy at NAVSSES hasn't quite grasped that yet. Heck, how can the Navy understand that concept, when it keeps promoting kids that have lived the sheltered life, and are quickly placed into a directorships position with so much money to boot?

It's similar to the killing fields of Cambodia, where children were murdering thousands of innocent adults. Young adults quickly promoted sans merit (an assault weapon) soon find's out that they can get away with all sorts of anti-socials mannerisms, and it is these same young managers who create a fear factor upon others within their area of influence, thus stifling creativity, and instead they build an atmosphere of waiting to be told what to do next, much like a puppy dog anticipating when the stick will be thrown.

Gauly! Slap-me-five with tongue lapping - Daugh...

And as proof that you cannot trust the Government to do right is recent article in the local papers May 7, 2008. The article was titled "FBI raids U.S. Special counsel offices of Scott Block. Block was responsible for protecting whistle-blowers from reprisals. Here was the top guy in charge of protecting the little guy from abusive managers, but instead he decided to run his own inquisition. Does his form of abuse also go on at NAVSSES? Absolutely, why do think the employees fear reporting abusive managers? My last manager when he could not go after me because I retired/left in disgust, he went after one of my close coworker. He did that by harassing him for frivolous status reports, and then he trumped up charges on his annual evaluation. One of the charges fielded was that the field reps did not like the co-worker. Can you imagine? Since when does a field rep have to like you to get his work done? Another comment was that he failed to recently look at a spreadsheet. A spreadsheet of a dozen others, all of them saying the same thing, who's on first? It was as if this manager was rooting through anything he could find to fail this person, to degrade. It was obvious that this manager was stewing from my letter that I sent to the Captain, and his actions against the co-worker were nothing more than retaliations.

And once such comments are documented on your work evaluation report, upper management (meaning the Captain and Director) cowardly sanctioned that the accusations could not be altered and would remain in your records. How's that on someone's self esteem? Normalcy would indicated that the proper course would be to find some way to rectify the knife in the back feeling, wouldn't you say? Creativity immerges from a series of mistakes, but at NAVSSES punishment is the order of the day, the rack, the iron maiden, the sinking feeling in a dark dungeon.

Did anything the manager wrote about the co-worker on his PARS really matter, when compared to the persons ability to get his projects moving and installed? A recently hired woman that has never completed a single project develops a spreadsheet of ongoing projects, and she receives a huge award and a promotion. While the co-workers with a history of outstanding work getting his projects installed year after year, and he has long ago developed spreadsheets of his projects detailing expenses and status, receives a slap to his moral and a threat of demotion. The disgrace of what some managers get away with at NAVSSES is long overdue for an investigation by the Better Business Bureau and other such investigating departments of Standards of Conduct, outside of the military.

INSTILLING FEAR IF LOOKING
AT THE INTRANET

To enlighten the public of some of the fears that some supervisors and or managers impose on subordinates, I'll mention one type that I found most appalling. It involved instilling fear in researching the Intranet for anything except work related subject matter. Now, we all know that most of us have scanned around the Intranet for all kinds of information including an occasional funny here and there. But to see individuals that were so scared to look at something trivial was mind-boggling. I have to say that I found quite a few of them who would not look at the Intranet for fear of losing their job. The answer I got was, "I'll look at it when I get home." And yet in other areas, the employees were checking out the Intranet for sports, laughing their head off from a cartoon or whatever and some thought nothing to print out the daily news or sports section everyday. Extremes existed at both ends.

One of my managers let us know that we were being watched. That information had some of the guys unplugging their computers from the network just so they could feel secure during such brief moments. Some even went so far as to install their own scrambling systems and there were other tricks used to circumvent being big brother watched.

All the while some of the employees were working in fear everyday others openly watched sports, read the news, downloaded stock figures and scanned comical videos and such. These were the morons that were causing much of the networking system to come to a crawl much of the time. Did management ever say anything about? No way.

WAR VETERANS

And what about the war veterans, the people, who sacrificed it all, only to be told that they did not qualify for the promotion? According to the Navy's way of promoting; some young person recently out of college, some how seemed to have much more knowledge and insight, verses a war veteran with vast knowledge into the workings of a ship, or anything mechanical or even how to supervise people.

Is this how, we repay the veterans, by keeping them down, like one ex-war veteran I knew personally? He was a great friend and an expert on shipboard switchboard system and much more. And because he understood switchboards so well, his manager/supervisor kept him on travel fifty percent of the time. Needless to say, all of his constant traveling took a toll of his marriage, which ended up in a divorce.

It wasn't until my friend; the war veteran complained about the others in his department, that some of his co-worker engineers were made to travel. And you guess it, some of the engineers faked sick leave to get out of them. The majority of the phony engineers were eventually promoted up into supervisory and managerial positions, so much for knowing your job. Anytime, you want details I'm sure I can go back to my friend for the specifics. And the Navy is presently on a quest to eliminate the very people that know the ship systems, the technicians. Go figure.

Oh, before I forget about my friend, he was kept at a GS-11 rate up until roughly a year before he left in frustration, from all the retaliations his supervisor was placing on him, for complaining about a promotion. A kid recently out of school moves right up, and when you're a war veteran, the Navy walks all over you keeping you down. How shameful is that from an organization top heavy with managers making $149K plus outrageous bonuses? That's four times the average yearly salary of the working American. And that doesn't include the insurance coverage and medical benefits.

Show me the products — what are the taxpayers receiving for such huge waste of monies — especially when Social Security cost of living is only 2.5 % cost of living increases. And that's based on a reduced retirement income without the locality cost of living added. Fair — I think not.

DISCRIMINATION AND EQUIVALENT DEGREE

It's all a different kind of discrimination, regardless, the Federal government needs to revise the definition of what is and isn't discrimination in the work place. Not everyone was afforded a perfect home where Mommy and Daddy pays and nurtures the child through college. Some of us were called off to war and others had dysfunctional families or none at all, preventing them from receiving a college education.

Where does the Navy come off focusing solely on the child with a piece of paper, especially the children that were born with a silver spoon? And what about those individuals that can only afford to take a few courses after they have been working for some time? Not many of these individuals can find the time to complete all the required courses to receive a full-fledged college degree, especially since many of the colleges filled up requirements to receiving one their degrees, with ridiculous non-engineering electives. Does the Navy suggest telling that person that they wasted their time taking all those courses?

The combining of a smattering of college course credits was initiated by the military, to assist those individuals that had a history of constantly relocating, from state to state due to their military commitments. If the person had the core engineering courses, the remaining electives could be made up by giving that person credit for past work experiences. Hell, I had a four-year apprenticeship worth more than four major engineering courses. But NAVSSES turned a blind eye to my past experiences just so some incompetent could reign in my place. If you don't believe me – then please explain how the past directors allowed the place to whittle down to practically nothing? There are so few working on anything serious at NAVSSES that it doesn't make sense to keep funding its existence.

The only people that I saw who received an equivalent college degree from the Navy were those individuals who had a relative in the business and or the person was a minority. Yes I said minority, and he was reclassified as an engineer to show that the organization was not discriminating. There was one other guy that I knew, who received an equivalent degree and from what I know, he was in the front line of lecturing, teaching that sort of division, so it wasn't much for him to zero in on exactly what few additional courses were required. He took the bare minimum, and the Navy put him in for an equivalent engineering degree.

And then there was a director with a degree in Chemistry, who was written up for an engineering degree reclassification, without having to take any additional schooling. It was all done so that a woman could be a shoe-in for the directorship position. Oh, I forgot there was a quota that had to be met.

In my case, I had a lot more college courses under my belt to qualify or be rated as an engineer, but the people reviewing my list of courses were not giving me credit, for any of my management courses, my accounting degree, my four year apprenticeship, or even the fact that I was for years in the business of running a web design business. Web designing requires extensive computer programming; something I guarantee a good majority of the engineers working at NAVSSSES had very little training in. Not to mention understanding the complexities of metals and tolerances that I learned from my background as a toolmaker. Unless you've spent time in the trenches of machinery construction, you have no concept of how things truly work. Accounting by the way is one of those engineering electives, go figure. And besides, the Personnel indicated that I only required one more course to qualify, and that they would put in for the equivalent degree if the manager would submit a letter.

That manager was Dick Willy, the first in a series of other supervisors and managers that were derelict in writing the letter for me. Dick an ex-Navy Chief with no college degree, I can understand. Here again, why would he want to promote me when he himself never received a college degree? Like I said, the Navy is dead wrong in assuming that managers want to promote the very best.

As I'm writing this book, I saw on television where Gloucester County New Jersey has submitted a plan whereby individuals that have undergone an apprenticeship, like the one I went through via the shipyard, could qualify for twenty-five credits towards receiving their college degree. Also college credits may be earned for work experience if the student's jobs are related to fields of study or career goals and there's more. So, there you go, it takes a local county college to wake up to acknowledging that apprenticeships amount to something. I'm sure that there are many other colleges out there that provide the same benefits for past work experiences under the Cooperative Education Program. Anyway, I not only had a complex training in the apprenticeship for anything to do with metal, forging, casting etc. I also had tons of experience from working in the design division and more.

The Navy had such a plan to give credit for past experiences, but it only used it whenever it suited the manager, not the organization. A most basic benefit to acquiring the employees' loyalty and to boost productivity is to foster educational benefits, via a whole series of small awards for each classroom course completed, to guarantees of promotions for completion of specific curriculums. As it presently stands at NAVSSES, and other similar military organizations, they do not have a department setup to review an employee's achievements to make recommendations to said employee, as to where he needs to tweak his abilities, hence an award or a potential promotion.

Can you imagine how the moral would improve if, occasionally, an employee received a letter or an email, telling them how to elevate themselves for the betterment of the organization? Some letter that might say, "We see that you have all this past experience in submarine construction and so many college credits. From our analysis it appears that you only require two major electives to qualify to be reclassified as an engineer, accountant or whatever, with a guaranteed award upon completion and more.

Such an in-house management concern for his people via such notices of individual assistants can only improve the working atmosphere, verses the presently existing air of distrust (them against us) mentality. People need to know that they are working in a close-knit family-like atmosphere. In a close family, members often add encouragement, monetary assistance and such positive help. It can only make the employees want to work harder, offer ways to improve things and make them want to tell everyone of how great it is to work for NAVSSES. A tight-knit-family does not require a contract or letter of understanding.

NAVSSES might argue that there isn't funding for such personnel tasks, but how does it justify receiving funding for pie charts and huge awards for its managers? How much difference is there between what I just suggested for the working employee, and the assistance parents with little children receive sans any negativity? There are many such employee improvement suggestions to increase loyalty and such, but until NAVSSES receives true leadership – what can I say. As long as the directors view their world from the inside of a canyon they will never understand the big picture. In the directors mind they see themselves as standing at the peak of some mountain, which explains why they only see clouds (the fog of clarity).

Urban Outfitters is a company that moved into several of the abandoned shipyard buildings after they were refurbished. I had the pleasure of talking to some of the women working for Urban Outfitters. I have to tell you that not a single person had a negative thing to say about it. All of the designers had pretty much a large open cubical to work in without being constantly pressured for trivial reporting. Now - I understand that NAVSSES was working under a different set of circumstances, but to submit talented engineers and technicians to insults, ridiculous spreadsheets and pie charts that says what forty other such paperwork say is retarded. NAVSSES is in need of a director that can get his head below the clouds and communicates with his people. By communicating I mean writing it down wants and needs and following up. No one wants to hear another airless politician spewing promises.

Employee Appreciation Day amounted to standing in a very long line, as if we were captive prisoners in some concentration camp, for a hot dog, hamburger, a soda and 35 cent bag of potato chips. And when they had Ethnic Diversity Day I asked the Captain if was ok to wear my Roman soldier's outfit, "No, it's not appropriate for the event," I was told. Come the day of the event, the Captain appeared wearing her Japanese Kimono dress. I suppose a Kimono is standard dress code in Japan, I haven't visited the place lately. Thankfully, the day of the event turned out to be one of the hottest days of the year and dressed in iron gear would have been quite stressful. I do know of one engineer, who liked to come in everyday dressed in a Western outfit made from covered-wagon canvas pants, matching wrist gauntlets and cowboy hat. I was expecting to see his covered-wagon in the parking lot, but…

In my thirty plus years, I have never known of a manager that would take a personal interest in any of the subordinates, unless it was to elevate his own agenda. All of them would let us know their achievements and future goals, and they would turn away when it came time for one of the subordinates to speak. It doesn't make for a comfortable place to work knowing that the boss is deaf to an employee's issues.

PRIVATE VERSES NAVY CIVILIAN SALARIES

Somehow, the Navy always seems obliged to hire the mud headed paper brats, those with few synapse connections. If the Navy was so concerned about hiring engineers, they made little effort to hire the best at competitive salaries in my opinion. Existing records prove that the Navy engineering salaries far exceed what the private sector pays, for the same engineering services. As proof there are private sectors that only require less than ten engineers to design some of the tallest building in the world. And what about the handful of engineers that are designing rockets that can take tourist into space and back, or the engineers that are designing very clever one-man submarines. Like I said, with as many engineers that presently exist at NAVSSES they should have built a flying aircraft carrier by now. They can start with my concepts of a flying aircraft carrier which is viewable at my website under patents if they require a clue to get them started.

WHY AM I COMPLAINING?

I'm not denying that there were others including many engineers that were never promoted either. So why am I complaining? I am complaining because I wasted a lot of my own money and time to get educated. Only to be ignored time and time again for my efforts. It wasn't only the self-education to which I was ignored. I was ignored after authoring several complex technical manuals for high-pressure steam governor systems. I was ignored after two major aircraft carriers repairs that I was on for several weeks, where I rebuilt four engine rooms of governors while it was still steaming. I was ignored for designing the solid-state aircraft-fueling system the Navy has been using for near 20 years since their inception. That system has worked flawlessly ever since. There were so much more, including the fact that I was practically always rated highly satisfactory from my excellent working abilities, and knowledge of just about any ship systems subject matter, including my near perfect work attendance. Even when I was working in the shipyard, I was one of a handful that came in during the major holidays to complete a project. I even contributed more beneficial suggestions than anyone else in the shipyard.

And at NAVSSES, all on my own, I was instrumental in supplying articles about our department to the local Navy news. The name of the magazine, by the way, has changed several times since. I had engineering articles published in magazines such as Popular Science, a slew of patents and not to bore the reader, face it; I was a mover and a shaker. Plus there's no denying that I was the only person in our MACHALT section that provided several articles about our work for the Navy Base Sounding magazine. And not once was I ever asked to do so for the section. You would think that at least one of the over paid GS-13s in our section would have been required to do that. Heck, I could see that our section was dieing, and that the other departments or NAVSEA should have some understanding of what we do. If you don't advertise, who is going to know who you are or what you do.

So while the majority of the people working at NAVSSES were reading the news, sports, shopping, watching the stock market or playing some type of game on the Intranet, during any of my free time, I usually spent it researching computer programming and such technical issues.

Don't ever try to convince me that some guy that watches a ball rolling on the grass to end up in a sunken empty soda can, or that the guys that watches an oblong ball get thrown and hand carried between two polls, or guys that bounce a ball around some hardwood floor and toss it through a fishnet hanging basket and others such cat-ball mesmerizing people are creative let alone engineers to be proud of. To watch sports now and then for stress relieving is understandable, but to follow it twenty-four seven borders on a lower life form. I know because I watched cats and dogs do the same until the ball disappeared or was taken away. Engineers, I think not.

A BETTER WAY TO PROMOTE

Which brings to mind a concept that I had for promoting not only supervisors and managers, but it also includes the employees themselves. And that involves the employees' input. Sure why not, why can't the employees have a vote into who should be their boss? What's wrong with that? Wouldn't that make for a better working environment? After all, employees are not about to promote favoritism or stupidity or even promote someone solely based on a piece of paper, and all the other cheap shots the Navy presently uses.

Yeah, the Navy has a full-fledged directive regarding promotions, but everyone knows, that the Navy doesn't adhere to their own rules. Had they done so, the union, which won every case, would not have repeatedly challenged them.

On several occasions I published articles, and wrote letters to my personnel department suggesting a way to make the promotion process more fair and honest. I suggested that all applications be void of names, religion, sex, color, race, and so on, or any nuance that could identify the person. The person would send in his resume sans the above info and be given a code number. Then from all the applications received, a selection is made solely on the merits of the qualifications and work experienced documented on the application. The winning number is then posted on the Internet. The person selected would then be required to provide proof of their qualifications, and if that person's credentials are verified, they are it. It's that simple. An alternate method is to have one armed forces review applications from another armed forces, such as the Army reviews the Navy applications and vice verse.

But then again, there is one other method that the Navy fails to use to investigate a persons ability to supervise or manage. And that is to simply check the person's credit report. I know I mentioned it earlier. If a person has a bad credit rating, he could be afforded a chance to explain why his credit was low. Why would anyone promote some simple-minded kid recently out of college, a kid with no financial record keeping abilities to run a multi-million dollar management system? But go figure, the Navy does just that.

One other technique that would ensure the more qualified, is promoted, would be to have the co-workers have a percentage say, in whether or not a person is qualified. In other words, the manager's input would be given 'x' number of percentage points, background experiences, schooling and such are given so many points, and the employees or co-workers the remaining percentages of points, based on the persons ability that the co-workers are aware of. Co-workers know individual candidates much better than the managers know the applicants, because management is often isolated from the herd of workers. Crap, even input from some of the contractors about a person ability is better than the sometimes illegal phony methods the Navy presently utilizes.

None of the Navy departments I have repeatedly sent my promotion suggestion to; have taken on my idea even though they were published in several of the major military news magazines. Unless an idea comes from the top, it will never see the light – the top brass rarely removes some of its ear crud for fear of failure I suppose. You hear that Admirals. The Navy people can break dance around performance evaluations all it wants, but they will never be void of some manager's personal agenda. With my proposal promotional methods, the Navy can pretty much eliminate claims of discriminations, favoritism, etc. Come-on Navy, isn't it time to grow up? Keep up the favoritism skullduggery and someday there's going to a big-time investigation.

LOST TO THE UNION, AND YET

Sadly the same people at NAVSSES, the management higher ups, who lost to the union for the deceitful despicable way that they were promoting people, were all put in for fantastic huge awards that same year. Is there no shame in NAVSSES for such a shame? And what about the supervisors and manager that allowed the unlawful promotions to proceed? Why weren't they disciplined, a letter in their record perhaps? After all, if a supervisor can write up an employee with a letter in his record for recycling a filing cabinet that was marked for trash, why is it that the Navy still allows the GS-13 and 14 to get away with such illegal promotions and falsifying overtime and much more?

KILLED MANAGER

Just for some insight into what might happen again and it almost came to that – the manager in this case was killed. It didn't happen at NAVSSES, it happened at the manager's home. NAVSSES knows whom I'm referring to, only that the manager's son got to him first. It wasn't a secret that the questionable disliked manager was a real nasty person in his department, everyone there hated the way this manager monitored every five minutes of what each person was doing – anal retentive (kind of like my last boss). Did anyone from NAVSSES say or doing anything about this guy? Maybe tell him to ease up, see a psychologist, or take a vacation, nope, nothing. I suppose his son had some issue too. The manager's demise could have occurred at NAVSSES by…

No one openly applauded the cruel manager's death, but those who knew him breathed a shy of relief knowing he wasn't going to show up for work anymore. Sad, but true.

Now, had NAVSSES been listening to the subordinate employees things might not have been so tragic for the man. Counseling, a change of work or training in how to deal with people might have had some impact.

What I see happened to this manager, and why he behaved tyrannical towards his co-workers may have come about, because of the way NAVSSES implements unfair practices when it comes to promoting, handing out awards, recognizing achievers and so on. Yes, I've seen it often happen when someone doesn't get promoted or receive an expected award, that person can become one hell of a person to deal with. Sticks and stones can break my bones but to be overlooked for all of the above. Come-on NAVSSES?

Now had NAVSSES poled its people about the way they were being treated, supervised etc. things could have been a lot rosier at the workplace.

NAVSSES assumes in some sick kind of way that just because there is a priest, mullah or whatever in the building that the children must be safe. I think some parents believed that one, just like the Navy wants to believe that if they pay their managers $149K and lavish them with huge annual bonuses, that they would play fair and honest.

SOME WASTE

Toilet paper waste:
It irked me to no end, whenever I saw a dozen or so printed copies of some sports article strewn on the floor in one of the water closet dumping stalls. If it wasn't about sports it was about the stock market. I can't imagine what was lying on the floor in the ladies room. At times I would count roughly twenty or thirty sheets of paper. What a waste of good copier paper and an eye opener into what the majority of the workers were more in-tune with. It was these same people who were slowing down the whole networking system by locking on to streaming stock feeds, and yet not a single spineless Captain or director mentioned about the abuse via one of their speeches or some Email. I'll bet in a private organization this kind of waste doesn't go on.

There was one issue in the paper waste that I found interesting. It was that the majority of the people doing the paper wasting were the new young recruits'. The older salts I suppose tend to be more in tune with hard times and understand the value of saving. This might also explain why the young want to be paid more for less work.

Moving cubicles and buildings waste:
Often, whenever we had a new manager in our department, he would have us move from one cubical to another, so as to appear as if to he was doing something important. Somehow moving people one or two cubicles is suppose to make the department work more efficient, never mind that whenever your supervisor needed to see you for anything, that he always sent you an Email. So what's the big deal if your one cubical or eight cubicles away?

Moving people around unless they wanted to move is always upsetting to that person. People tend to settle into a nest sort of speak within their environment. Moving them to a new location requires that they rebuild that same security that they originally had. Often the favored ones seem to get the bigger booths, and the least likable might have a windowless spot, bad lighting or a stanchion within their space.

I doubt that there is a single manager or supervisor at NAVSSES that can show, that work output improved because of such annual musical chairs break-dancing. It was just some boss pissing on his subordinates, to show his people, who was the boss and nothing else.

And then the most wasteful money was spent having to relocate us from one building to another. And this was done quite often. For a while, it almost seemed like every two years or so, our department or organization moved into another building. The buildings we just vacated were often freshly painted, and we were all issued new furniture in them. Much of that new stuff was left behind. We were told that we would be getting new stuff, but this was new stuff we were leaving behind. Our unused furniture was then trucked off as waste, or sold as surplus at a penny to the dollar. And no – no other department moved into what we just left behind.

Not only was nice furniture left behind, tons of research material would end up in the dumpsters too along with personal records about everyone in the place, like sick leave slips, Naval messages, confidential technical manuals and just about anything some enemy might want to know about the Navy. Yes - I saw stacks of sick leave slips wrapped in rubber bands and it wasn't the Naval messages that were so bothersome as the tech manuals I saw tossed into dumpsters. I look back, and I had a jackass of a Captain place a letter in my records for faxing a message with nothing confidential on it except for the word confidential, imagine that. And thank you Mr. Warty my super.

Such building moves wouldn't have been so bad, if we were a bunch of African hyenas moving out of one flea infested den to another freshly painted clean den.

In one of the buildings, I can even recall all of us being issued a complete computer desk in a kit form – assembly required. We were all to assemble our units, or with the help of others if you were a paper engineer without a clue. When the units were completed, we could lock in our new computers when we left work at night. They were beautiful expensive furniture sets. No more than two to three months after we assembled our new desks, we were told that we would be moving to another building with all new furniture. Now I don't begrudge having new furniture, but this was clearly waste, fraud and abuse by our managing department. Time and time again, I saw similar mismanagement occurring throughout my near forty plus years with the Navy. I'm sure; various military institutes have very similar mismanagement problems. It was all part of that mind set of helping out the economy. Spend, spend, spend, and never mind trying to save the taxpayers some money. Or better yet, using that money to promote more people.

If the Navy really wanted to save capital investment funding in NAVSSES, they should move into some of the buildings right across the Delaware River into the City of Camden, New Jersey. But no, it's more prudent for the Navy to dance about the closed ex-Navy Shipyard, moving from one building to another. Once a building was totally refurbished, various departments move into it and utilize the building for few short years until another building was refurbished. And each time the transition occurred, someone in the upper management received an award for having done a great thing. Get real – move to Camden and you'll really cut back on rental fees, help that city and much more. I believe it was the director making those improvident decisions. At one time when ships were being dry-docked for repairs and such, it made sense to have the technical departments in close proximity. Today with no ships around – none of it makes any sense to continue to remain in Philly.

Computer Waste:

While I'm on computers I might as well mention the ridiculous price of five billion dollars, for the rental of the desk or laptop computers and a contract for the same for the next five years. The cost was roughly $450 per month per person depending on the model computer and the types of software they had. Can you imagine just how ridiculous that cost is? At that outrageous price rate, the Navy could have owned the computers and better ones at that. Some politician or an ex-Navy person had to have had his sticky fingers in that contract. People listen again - that's five billion dollars, can you imagine how much of that money could have put to better use in a dead city like Camden, New Jersey or some other needy city?

Almost immediately after we got the new computers, a program was implemented to block all personal Email websites so that you couldn't email a loved one at home or for whatever. But cell phones were ok. So if you didn't own a cell phone you were out of luck. Isn't that a bitch? I never bothered to own a cell phone, but everyone around me had one and used them everyday for hours at a time. If they couldn't call from inside the buildings, they would hang around outside. Fair, I think not. Once again, the Navy demonstrated that it favored the waste the time employees, more so over the honest hard worker. Working for the Navy is not exactly all that you could be.

Why not block sports sites like porno sites are blocked, and what about blocking investment stock streaming sites? Those sites don't have anything to do with engineering or Navy stuff.

Seminar Waste:
For technology to advance you need to diversify frequently. And that means advancing those individuals without degrees, and recognizing those that made the effort to better them selves. They deserve some preference. And I don't mean, making the employees take those ridiculous childish moronic seminars that amounted to nothing, on the guise that they will aid in the persons ability to be promoted. The only people making money on those stupid boring talk seminars were the contractors. The same people which sold them to the Navy, as if the people attending them were going to benefit somehow. I'll bet if there was an investigation they might find collusion between the, Director and or some manager, showing favoritism to an ex-Navy civilian person selling them the phony seminar. After all, if NAVSSES is suppose to be some humongous engineering facility, why the crap is the place paying outrageous fee for child like seminars. Why not refresher courses on engineering stuff, verses those stupid technical writing or how to deal with people yawning courses.

Hammer:
Just before I retired, let's see, there was at least four people in the chain of command, I mean the chain of stupidity that had some dealings with the funding in our section. That's one section of a multitude of sections/departments. One in the line was a recently promoted individual, and then there was my ex-supervisor (somehow he was still in the accounting loop), then our accountant followed by the manager placing his signature on my document for a purchase under a couple of hundred bucks. And it still hadn't left our section for someone to enter my purchase into a computer for the

purchasing department to act on it. That's one GS-14, two GS-13, and two GS-12 and I'm not even mentioning the secretary and slew of people in purchasing. Now people-this is a prime example of that $3000.00 hammer costing up to $30,000.00 and in the end, the Navy gets a stick and a rock. The string to tie the rock and the stick together is extra, and it doesn't come with a claws or nail-puller that's extra too.

Managers! What managers? They're all thieves hidden in a line-dancing samba labeled the chain of command. Nothing can get done until everyone in the samba line signs the service request. The service request is a piece of paper to buy something. This is one of the main reasons why the managers fear allowing the employees to work from home. My God! Who would they manage to justify their high salary?

PLATFORM OFFICE

We had a huge message center; the Platform office as it was called, that frankly, just shuffled naval messages around. I say huge, because the Navy has a bad habit of sub dividing up departments. Maybe it was just NAVSSES. Subdividing was done, so that they could justify more phony promotions, more Chiefs than Indians. You see, ships come in classes, amphibians, surface combatants, carriers etc., but for some odd reason, the Navy felt each class required its own specific chief to handle what amounted to the same message. On our organizational chart it was further broken up into ship systems, such as pumps, electrical, propulsion, controls, etc. It was as if the management was running the Olympics with orthopedic shoes with the department store price string still attached, hobbling both shoes. Determining who did what at NAVSSES became gray as the color of the ships them selves.

Com-on Navy show everybody a copy of a Surface Combatant message and one from an Amphibian class ship. A message is a message, when you subdivide a department it becomes difficult for one section to know what is going on in another section – miss communications. It's like the Navy trying to communicate with the Army and vice verse. Pretty dumb, wouldn't you say, and the Iraq war proved it?

Even if NAVSSES wanted to keep the Platform office subdivided according to ship classes, why not at least list the ships where each department section was responsible for, clearly visible within the department somewhere. Put it on the door entrance or somewhere on the cubical booth, so that a stranger/visitor can locate who he's looking for. Even the Email addresses provided no clues about who did what in the platform office. Efficiency - there wasn't any. Once, I walked into what I thought was the area responsible for a particular class of ship, and I was told to go here and go there. And none of this was listed within the in-house emailing system. Wouldn't that be nice to see whose cog over what ships, so I knew whom to contact if I had a question.

Oops, I forgot, you couldn't ask the people in the platform office a question, because you would only get the run around. "Did you try contacting the field reps in Norfolk?" And no one in that department could tell me exactly what series of command addresses, were required for any of my messages. It was always a guessing game at best. And these were supposed to be the people that were often promoted much higher than the rest of the technical codes, and yet many of them could not answer my most basic message writing questions. Field reps, home ports, command in charge, squadron and so on, nothing, I couldn't get nothing useful but fluff came out of that overpaid department. If it weren't for many of us keeping copies of previous messages, we would have floundered for days to assemble a Naval message. Messages, that one out of ten, could have been issued more efficiently via an email.

By the way, much of the break down of departments into sub classes of ships and component sub system was to justify more supervisors/promotions. Which in turn, if you have too many supervisors you can then ask for more managers, and so on all they way up to the overpaid directors, who falsely claim to be managing so many higher ranking do nothing numb nuts, hence, the reasons for their ridiculous unjustified pay scale and bonuses.

So here was this, push message papers around platform office, that should know all the silly nuances of writing a message, such as the chain of command and shipyards etc that goes on a message, and yet we all had to learn how to write messages. Make one mistake and the message was rejected, and you had to start all over, which could take as long as another week waiting for your chain of commands to review and sign it first.

Ah, the chain of command. Let me say something about that. Everything starts from your immediate supervisor signing your masterpiece message, which could have taken a good part of a week to put together with much sphincter quivering anticipation to ensure correctness. Then it goes to the manager, from there the message is sent to the technical code responsible for the specific piece of equipment, God forbid if there is more than one technical code that has to review your message. If everything is ok, it goes to the message center (the platform office). Oh, I left out the secretary. Each and every one of those people reviewing your message had Carte blanch to rewrite it according to their whims. And trust me, we had a ton of managers and supervisors that were weenies, what can I say—ass-hole rewriters. These weenies just wanted to show that they could say the same thing in your message in another way.

Now we use Email and it rarely if ever gets edited or rewritten, unless it was to estimate a job, and then the supervisor added his expenses and whatever. So what would have taken a couple days to write a message and send off, often took anywhere from three to four weeks before it was sent. By then, many of the ships requesting assistant often solved it themselves. Basically - the FU salute...

Ah, but wait, before a ship can fix or repair its own mechanical problem, it required confirmation from one of NAVSSES technical godly codes, that it was ok to proceed. "The Mother may I syndrome." And before that could happen, the technical code engineer often had to consult one of the technicians who tended to be more familiar with the equipment. You see—technicians were often ex-navy chiefs, shipyard workers or personnel with on-hands experience. In other words, these were the people that really understood how the piece of equipment operated, and they knew how to troubleshoot it should a glitch in the equipment arise. Should the technician not know anything about the piece of equipment, the engineer would call the manufacturer for assistance. So what was the purpose of having an overpaid engineer, when the technician could have resolved the ships problem, thereby increasing operating efficiency and lowering costs? But no, the Navy wants to do just the opposite—they want to eliminate as many of the technicians as they can and hire more inexperienced clueless engineers.

And no, the Navy couldn't and did not designate that the secretaries be responsible for message writing, which would have freed up the engineers and technicians to do what they do best, or better yet, have the over-paid message center write the messages. Even after computers were in use for some ten years, we were not allowed to communicate with the Navy fleet via a simple Email. Nope—Emails were too simple to use. And shortly after Emails came into being, the Navy implemented a new computer program for sending Naval Messages, what bunch of crap that was. It was even more difficult to use than the first DOS operated one, which we had come to know and understand before. The designers of the new message program had no concept of simplifying it so that much of the information was automatically filled in. For instance, if I had to send a message to a specific ship telling them that I would arrive on such a date, the program should have been able to fill in all the sub divisions of commands, and the shipyard division that needed to know etc. period.

If the wasteful Navy wants to continue using the draconian massage system to relay a message to a ship, that one of the technicians is arriving to troubleshoot/assess their problem; then the Navy should utilize the overpaid secretaries and or the message center to write them. Anyone of us in the technical fields or project managing should have been able to just Email the message center of what we wanted, and they in turn should be the department that formulates the message and sends it out. After all, the platform center better understands the multitude of shipyard, ships and the various departments calling numbers. But no, the Navy expected everyone to be doing everyone else's job.

Folks, I didn't mind writing messages, they were just another challenge and nothing more. Messages from the technical codes should only spell out the solutions to a problem and nothing more. The Platform office should then take those messages, add all those that need to know commands and send it off. Traveling and visiting messages should be abolished and done via an email.

CHASING AFTER FUNDING

At one point when things were looking a bit iffy for NAVSSES, we were all asked to go after funding in Washington too. What a bunch of chicken-shit managers time that was. Can you imagine, here was my GS-13 supervisor and my GS-14 manager with no balls to go to Crystal City in Washington D.C. and publicly speak in front of some guys for funding. When NAVSEA Washington was getting inundated with so many of us coming over to do a soft shoe of our project, they finally relented and went back to designating just one person do the soft shoe. Actually, none of us GS-12s were trained in whom to see or to contact at NAVSEA, and instead, we were left to wander about Crystal city asking questions. Not the best way to do business.

Sadly, this mass blind chasing after funding, all of a sudden stopped at about the same time, that we had a GS-13 promotion in our department. And suddenly, all my work relating to begging for funding at Crystal City and getting to know some of the people there ceased. The writing was on the wall; from now on, the new supervisor in our section was elected to represent us in Washington.

I might also include that this was about the same time, that NAVSEA was looking to slash some 40% of their workforce. The reduction at NAVSEA was long overdue since it was obvious; that every time that I was there I rarely found my contact person in their office. Most of them, I had to hunt down in the Mall that was located in the basement or first floor. My contacts were either shopping or at one of the eateries.

Did our newly promoted main-man do a good job? I think not, otherwise, we wouldn't have atrophied to degree that the department did after he took control, from lack of funding. The guy was new recently out of college and you guessed it, he knew very little about our projects. Shortly after that downfall, another individual recently out of college was placed into that position of representing our MACHALT department in Washington. And as usual, the young recent graduate quickly advanced to a GS-14 position without competition. Fair — I think not, because the rest of us with some fifteen plus years in the business weren't even given a chance to prove ourselves.

Had our organization had an atmosphere of a team playing, the rest of us wouldn't have been left in the dark about our funding contacts in Washington. You would think that whenever a supervisor or manager had to visit someone in Washington, that they would have taken an underling with him, as a way of insuring that the business stays strong with a solid foundation. Instead, the managers at NAVSSES practice a form of secrecy, like some lion hunkering down on a kill. It was if they were mumbling to themselves that, "If I tell them too much, they might know what I know, and then I won't look as important. I have to keep my contacts and where I get funding from in Washington a secret, that way, only I can go to Washington whenever I want to wallow away from the boring office, and then I can put in for some overtime too. Yeah, that's the ticket." That was the way I perceived our supervisors and managers, grubby creepy trolls.

WASTEFUL TRAVEL ORDERS, PURCHASE ORDERS AND WEBSITES

If there ever were three areas that caused many headaches and wasted time (and by the way, time costs money), it was in writing messages, filing travel orders and writing up a purchase order. That's three areas of paperwork at NAVSSES to which there isn't a single person can truly argue that they enjoy having to do.

And why is that? I already mentioned the Platform office and the ridiculous message writing fiasco. In this day and age of text messaging, emails and cell phones, why is the Navy still bent on using such backwards systems to communicate with a ship? Forget it, because I could mention a slew of what is wrong with the message writing system that the Navy still adheres to.

So back to the other two wasteful systems, travel orders and purchasing requests. For starters, like many of the departments that were created at NAVSSES, to handle specific jobs, such as purchasing, travel order and writing messages, does it make any sense to then ask each person at NAVSSES, to write their own messages, write their own travel order and or to write their own purchasing request, when there exist departments that do exactly that function. An organization working in harmony, NAVSSES certainly is not.

If I were still working in the MACHALT department at NAVSSES, where my job was to project manage a series of projects, I should not have to jump through hoops writing travel orders or purchase orders. I should be doing what I get paid for, managing.

What NAVSSES asks of the people to do is to do the secretaries work, the platform office's job, the purchasing peoples job, the travel people's job and so on. In the end, my travel request or my purchase order ends up costing the taxpayers a small fortune each time.

Yes, I could easily do their job. But is it right, anymore than is it right that NAVSSES has us practically emptying out or own wastebaskets? Funny isn't it, how the management wants everyone to understand everyone else's job sort of speak, but then they pick and chose who can handle job orders and those projects that are guaranteed, to get the special one promoted, sans honest competition?

No my friend, if you want efficiency, and the job done right every time then don't ask each person, to do everyone else's job. It's that simple. Not only do you eliminate tons of wasted paperwork, and you save time, time that can be used to better address a ship's urgent request.

You don't believe me? Try asking anyone that has traveled, what's the first thing he has to do before he can even start answering some of his backed up email? It's simple, he turns on his computer and he starts entering his travel expenses and putting in his overtime. By the time, he gets to answer any of his emails; at best it's late that evening, or he answers them the next day or two. When actually, the people at travel should have already done much of his travel information for him. In this day and age, there is no reason, why some hotel in Jabip cannot email directly to NAVSSES, the information requested about a person's stay. And the same can be done with car rentals, plane tickets, etc.

As it presently stands, travelers enter all their information through a personal computer, followed by a series of paper copies along with copies of receipts. Travel then calculates what you should get and processes you paperwork. None of it makes sense with today's technology? And the place is crawling with mind-boggling engineers can you imagine? No one is thinking about saving anything.

If not the travel department handling all the paperwork, then travel orders and expense reporting for such, should sit squarely on the secretaries' lap, and the department in charge of travel should handle them when the secretaries' can't do the work. In other words, no one at NAVSSES has taken the bull by the horns and made a sensible managerial decision regarding such mundane issues. Expensive professionals are presently doing, what I call secretary's work. So much for intelligent decision-making by the Captain, while watching the stock market for his retirement, where are the decision makers, "Show me the money," as they say?

Traveling to distant shipyards by the way was one of those big time wastes of money, especially, when you take into account the vast amount of ways that two people, or groups of people, can communicate via present day technologies. At a time when traveling has gotten to be expensive and time consuming, it made no sense back then and even less sense today to continue the practice. Think of the fuel savings and the reduced air pollution by utilizing video conferencing.

I might also mention that some of the traveling excursions were, how you say, illegal, in the sense that they were carried out solely to use up funding, either from an overpriced project or for some other wasteful cause. I knew of one individual who was sent from Navy base to Navy base, coast-to-coast, just to use up the money that was allocated for another ship that happened to be deployed. And then there were supervisors and managers in my department, which were traveling not so much for business, but to visit distant relatives, to put in claims for over time, and for phony travel expenses and or for a nice vacation like to Hawaii.

I don't begrudge someone a get-away now and then, but when it's the same managers or supervisors repeatedly traveling to paradise Islands and such places, something's wrong. Around the office it was common to hear of managers and supervisors taking golfing excursions verses being on travel for work issues. Yes, there have been many managers who switched places so that one manager can have a day off to be with his family in places like Hawaii, or in San Diego visiting museums, meanwhile the other manager covers for vacationing other. I believe the Navy has a term for this kind of travel abuse; it's called "Port and Starboard".

For some manager to let's say travel to Mayport, Florida, like the person I knew, to check on the field reps regarding some project seems asinine, considering the fact that, he could have done it via Emails, digital camera images of the site and via video conferencing. And then to make himself appear as if he went there to inspect and to do some serious work, the manager would then either contact one of his subordinates back at NAVSSES via a phone call or an email requesting, "Why this or that wasn't so and so taken care of?" All of which could have been done like I mentioned via a phone call or email. By the way, the person most likely to get the nasty gram was usually the person less likely to fight back. But the vacationing manager in sunny Florida understood that by hitting the lowest rung, the rest of the people above him will get the message, that the manager was out there checking on everyone's projects. Now, had the Captain asked some of the subordinates if the manager or supervisor was deserving of an award, I doubt that the abusive traveling manager would have received anything.

In my department when one of our guys wanted to travel to Hawaii to check on one of his projects, he was quickly denied. But when a young college woman wanted to go to Hawaii, well no problem, here take the other more experienced woman in our department with you, so she can show you around. Suddenly the manager had money for the two women to go to Hawaii, even though one of them was going along as a chaperon, but not for one of the guys with some serious project to inspect there was no funding. Crap, when I traveled anywhere, I went alone. I didn't need someone to hold my hand. I guess it's one of those girly things, like when they have to go to the bathrooms in twos.

The two women traveling together is one of those prime examples where the manager wanted to impress the girlies that he can be generous. But to the elderly guy with work to investigate, he was told to get lost.

Speaking of some women getting special perks, there was one who thought she had positioned herself as the go between the Port Engineers, and the rest of us within our department. It's one of those silly ways that a person can set themselves up for a promotion, by demonstrating that they have some kind of gift for gab, or whatever with some other remote entity like the Port Engineers. It's not much different, than the way supervisors and managers, try to keep the subordinate dumb, about the people working at NAVSEA or isolating them from funding. Anyway, one day, this woman came up to me, to tell me, that I had contacted one of the Port Engineers and to never to do that again. "Next time you need to talk to one of the Port Engineers, you're to contact me and I will get in touch with them."

"What? Is she nuts?" Like I can't pickup the phone to contact one of the Port Engineers regarding one of my projects? I just ignored her, and contacted them whenever I wanted. But it demonstrated just how the people at NAVSSES are placed into such situations to get ahead, by creating these ridiculous chains of nothings, just so that they could justify a promotion. And it seemed to be working for her, because this woman didn't seem to have any trouble what so ever in traveling. Were they necessary travels? Not really, because she had no qualms about asking others if she could travel in their place. A day or more out of the boring office, a place to smoke and drink, meet new people, sit around while visiting the sites, the smell of a new rental car, a fresh new hotel room, paid dinners, Oh my, who doesn't want that, plus questionable overtime?

And that isn't all, there's tons of over-time a traveler can put in for, after-all, who's checking. For example, there was this Black engineer, a big dude, as were his testicles, which put in for roughly $120 per day plus living expenses, while in a hotel in Bahrain for some twenty days. When actually, the Black engineer was riding the ship in the Persian Gulf the whole time. His travel amounted to several thousands of dollars. Had travel not looked into the bogus false claims, the guy would have gotten away with it? Was he dismissed for attempted theft – of course not, he only had to pay it back, but he did get to keep all that overtime he claimed. No way to check that. I'll mention more about this Black person later.

I would like to recount a job I had located in Subic Bay, Philippines while I was still working at the Navy shipyard. I have to tell you about some of the guys that I met at the Navy shipyard. I wasn't there goofing off all day, I did get some work done while I was there. Anyway, I got to meet the superintendent of the machine shop and we got into some friendly discussions regarding generalities about where I was from and so on. During the conversation, he mentioned that he knew one of the guys from my tool making shop back home in Philly. It seems the guy, James, was told that if he served a couple of years in the Philippines, he was almost guaranteed a Superintendents position back home. So Jiminy took the job, and when he returned to the states they made him Superintendent of the machinery shop in Philadelphia.

During our conversation, the Superintendent went on to ask me if I wanted to work in Subic, and he guaranteed that I could make some serious money. More money than I could ever make back in Philly. He went on to explain how it works. He would work one week while I was off to do what ever I wanted. Then I would cover for him the following week. We would both put in for 16 hours a day everyday. Should anyone call for us, the person covering would tell him, that I was out on one of the ships. Sounds pretty cool – all that easy money and more than enough vacation time off. Plus he said, "Look at all the cheap sex and maid service I could have while stationed there." Hookers cost ten bucks for the whole day, and there was a crap load of them always hanging around the Navy base.

It all sounded good, but I had so much cow manure at home to deal with from my girlfriend, Mary, with all her problems, and Mom with her crap load of children. The thought was tempting. The Superintendent went on to say, that some of the guys sent their kids back to the states when they got to be teenagers, because it was too easy for them to get into trouble with all the cheap flesh around – especially for the boys.

So there you go – who is watching the big wigs overseas? I understand from people who knew James, they told me that when the shipyard closed that he started a landscaping business. Boy, what happened to being Mr. Big shot businessman?

Websites:
If there was a website to put together for one of the NAVSSES departments, rather than look within, they failed miserably. Instead, what they continued to do was to pay millions to an outside contractor to put one together for them. Just like it squandered millions to contractors, for complex databases to organize some of our projects that never materialized, to anything useful. Even the way, that we had to enter our travel expenses to get reimbursed was antiquated, it was more like something created by a person of yesterday's computer intelligence. There were so many engineers working at NAVSSES, and you can't tell me that one of them would not have enjoyed creating a travel expense program. I was pretty damn good at understanding website programming, but…

Not only was the travel website crappy and difficult to figure out, much of it didn't make any sense. Captain, director and managers must have been a bunch of blank headed thinkers. By that I mean, where was their input, or what about the employees input?

WHAT IS NAVSSES?

NAVSSES is not a technology and research center, it's more of a CRAPTOLOGY center. And who was the Navy idiot moron, who labeled it, The Naval Surface Warfare Center? Thanks for making the place a target for the Muslim Terrorist. The place is not a Warfare Center; no one in the place plans any war strategy. Get real Navy. And to top that, the main gate to the Navy Base is left open for anyone to enter freely – especially the taxicabs and the oil tankers. Aren't the cab drivers predominately of Muslim decent? Not to discriminate, but the question needs some attention. And tough if the Muslims don't like it, this is war, and it wasn't that long ago, that all Japanese in America were sent to concentration camps.

In the United Kingdom, thankfully, they are finally cracking down on how, when, and where Muslims can utilize mosques, and they have been arresting the radicals for brainwashing young Muslims to becoming terrorist. Throughout the world, wherever there is a war going on and or massive deaths of innocent people and suicide killings, the predominant cause is because of radical Muslims, and no other radical religion. Notice that I said predominate cause. The UK is not the only European country waking up to radicals, Demark has stepped up to re-publish the Mohammed cartoon, and Italy has taken steps to deport many of the Arabs back to North Africa. Plus, if comedians, like Carlos Mancia, can joke about Arabs/ Muslims and stereotype them, I feel I can do the same, since it's only my opinion.

The title NAVAL SURFACE WAREFARE CENTER is the Navy creating the big lie by flying under the radar. When is the Navy going to wake up?

Promoted Engineers:
And now, I'll mention something about the demented concept of fighting a battle with a bunch of chiefs' (engineers) verses and army of worriers (technicians). The Navy should know better; that you can't row a canoe if you have more chiefs than Indians. The heavily feathered headgear gets in the way.

But seriously, dissention will exist throughout the organization, because of the disproportionate number of high rated engineers, doing exactly the same work or less as the technicians. Just about everyone that was an engineer was more fixated on getting on the Mummer's parade bandwagon of promoted clowns, than concentrating on doing an honest job. So in other words, anyone that was a GS-12, engineer, would feel cheated from a promotion as were the technicians, which felt even more hatred for the place, because the promotional announcements for the paperless technicians was even smaller.

If there was anything, creative coming out of the NAVSSES, it had something to do with toying around with 401K investments or sports figures. I can't tell you of how many of the so called engineers had their computer set up for streaming stock quotes, and others followed streaming sporting events.

WHAT MAKES NAVSSES EXPENSIVE TO OPERATE?

The cruxes of why it costs so much of what the Navy requires to be done or accomplished, is because of a slew of paperwork and documentations, along with a ridiculous organizational chart of top-heavy overpaid chiefs running the place. Chiefs do not make anything, except to ensure that they maintain status quo. And to do that, they look to promote a slew of underlings, thereby justifying their own higher GS position. What you end up having is too many fat cats with time to kill, playing solitaire on the computer to keep from falling asleep. As proof, I offer the organization the opportunity to show the American taxpayers, what it is that the place has designed, created or whatever for the Navy. Lockheed develops aircrafts; Martin develops way too much military equipment to list them all and so on. As far as I know, NAVSSES just offers repair advice and much of that information is gathered from the original equipment manufacturer, OEM. So why doesn't the Navy just circumvent NAVSSES and go directly to the shipyards for repair advice? Beats me...

And when it wasn't a promotion, it was a huge award somehow hidden within the project-funding estimate. Say again? You mean to say that someone over estimated the project, so that others could pocket some of the estimate as an award? I'm saying that if you were to investigate the residual, follow the money trail, there is none. So where did it go? Easy, stand back and take note of who's been getting the majority of the awards or the really big ones. Some of the people have recently retired. And not satisfied after retiring, they maintain their gluttonous mannerisms by working as an expert advisor for one of the major contractors.

Purchasing hang-ups:
Purchasing waste - where do I start? I guess you could say that the biggest complaint I heard was from the manager himself. A nitpicker when it came

to reviewing anyone's purchasing order. You could rewrite your purchase order exactly the way he dictated it should be written, and he would reject it again and again. Basically, the guy was paranoid about the purchasing order getting rejected, by some mystical other person beyond his control, in another department outside of NAVSSES control. So every word in the purchase order was read and re-read for accuracy umpteen times. In one of the contracts that he reviewed, the anal-retentive manager claims that he was able to save the government roughly $75,000.00. And when he did so, the manager for whom he had saved the money for angrily said, "What am I suppose to do with all this money, it's the end of the fiscal year?"

The contract and purchase order rejections were becoming so much of a problem, that many of the women who worked in the purchasing department were left in tears or frustrated. I'm not sure that the manager was ever demoted, but I was told that he was somewhat isolated and a woman promoted to the new vacated position.

It wasn't long before the newly promoted woman in the purchasing department was causing her own headaches, for the other subordinate women working there. It seems that several of the Black women were being overlooked in the promotions. So the Black women filed a discrimination complaint with the union's assistance.

No problem, the recently promoted purchasing manager retired to avoid the discrimination suit, and she came back to work in another department at NAVSSES, as a contractor advisor for purchase orders and writing contracts.

Boy, what ever happened to government workers that make such high salaries and with so much influence, taking a hiatus for like three to five years, before doing work for the same government department? There was also talk that the ex-purchasing manager had her favorite contractors when it came to awarding contractors. And it wasn't that difficult to control, whom gets what when it comes to awarding contracts. I've seen contractors lose a contract by not including a single key word in their bid. And it's their childish ploys, which purchasing at times uses to control the monopoly game of contracts and purchase orders.

The Navy is overdue to put out a very easy to use website, not the complex one presently in existence for all government buys. Many small businesses get too inundated with the complexity to navigate and register on any of the contracting sites, that they give up in frustration. No sane person buys like that. The material requested should be easy to understand as a catalog from Walmart and such. That way the Navy can ensure the cheapest prices, without all the hassles from a handful of savvy suppliers. Contracts for skilled workers can be similarly simplified.

The above mentioned complexity of maneuvering around the government contacting system is why the Navy/military then needs to deal with its own retirees returning to work as contractors. These are the same people that know how to manipulate the purchasing system to maximize their own personal profits. Wink, wink, "Hey Fred, it's Mike remember we used to work together anyway can you help me out?" Now is that fair to all others competing for some of that pie?

NASA does it better:
The NASA space technology, at least, seems to make some sense; after all, they have people's life in their hands. And I'm sure that after this book is published others will follow. Oh sure, NASA no doubt has it questionable problems, but I'll bet it's not as ugly as what has been going on at NAVSEA/NAVSSES. On the one hand, NASA produces a product that the whole world admires, whereas the Navy is basically block funded, and therefore it doesn't have to show results or make anyone proud. The Navy solution for accounting for the waste and abuse spending, created an anal retentive system that in the end produces a phony detailed money trail of nothing produced. But you can be sure as hell, that anyone can discover where the money was all spent - not. Much of it went to feeding the upper crust management system; if anyone from NAVSSES feels jubilant upon retiring - it's them the over paid fat cat managers.

$7000 AWARDS AND MORE

Awards, why do I keep harping on ridiculous awards? How do several $7000.00 awards for the managers and more every year sound, and for what? The Navy in my opinion keeps the awards secret, because they know that if others knew about them there would be a ton of citizens complaining. It isn't fair for the director and many of the managers to play head games with the lower rated hard working employees, while at the same time they pocket/steal money hidden as an award for themselves. To suggest secrecy of awards to ensure that NAVSSES operates effectively is nothing short of absurd. Try telling that to the private sector. And while your at it; try telling the public that such huge awards were given to managers managing a handful of professionals, professionals who do not need some jerk of a manager telling them how to do their secretarial level type jobs.

Also there's this, a coworker technician, who retired, informed me that when he was handed an award for $200 in an envelope, inside the same envelope was another check for $1200. That extra check was for an engineer in his department. When he took the mistaken check back to his supervisors, the supervisor stuttered, as he told him that he had marching orders to hand out larger awards to the engineers verses the technicians, even though they both carried out the same work. It wasn't those exact words but you get the jest of what ensued.

The true deservers of the awards are the same people who built the pyramid, and not the overpaid manager receiving even more than they can possibly spend. Beats me how the Captain, director and many of the managers can honestly look at themselves in the mirror every morning and say, "I truly deserved that award." I've often wondered how some managers and supervisors seemed to be receiving way too many awards until someone mentioned one of the tricks that they use to get them. You see if your one of the managers, you can write up just about anyone for an award. So what some of them did was to write awards for one another, time and time again. Which explains why the Navy is reluctant to publish which person receives what. I remember one person being put in for an award for not using any sick leave for the year. I never got one of those, and yet my leave record was impeccable including my tons of free time from arriving close to an hour and a half early everyday.

And there are many other such sneaky ways that specific individuals seemed to always get the awards or promotions. How is it that NAVSSES can find huge awards for directors and managers already making way over for what they do, while only a handful of subordinate employees were selected for the same? Bonus awards are supposed to be awarded when you create something above and beyond, and it should not be something that you expected year after like I saw happening at NAVSSES for doing your job. For gosh sakes, if I had all those years of producing highly satisfactory work, don't you think I should have at least been put in for one outstanding award, if not for a specific project – why not after 39 years of excellent service? Managers just have to hold the position to get the awards while the subordinates have to hop through fiery hoops to get one, if they are lucky.

Girls recently out of college were always, not sometimes, put in for special awards. You guessed it; it was so that the Navy could phony up the girls resume for an upcoming promotion. Once again, the award system is not an honest system; at least not the way the Navy implements it as I witnessed it.

Basically, what the Navy has is a bunch of pirates calling themselves managers and supervisors that find creative ways to loot the funding. It's an orgy of creative ways of denying as many subordinates as possible an award each year, thereby ensuring more funds remain at the end of the fiscal year to award themselves, the hard two-face managers. Yes, I've seen and I had it happen to me where a manager would deliberately hold back project funding, and at the end of the fiscal year when the money had to be used up, he would drop the funding excess on my lap to spend. Yeah right, you have one week to write up a purchase contract, and then get it approved sans a single rejection for the most trivial infraction, good luck. And then come evaluation time, well - you can imagine what the manager had to say…JACKASS. And there were other creative ways that managers could divert funding to ensure it would end up in the pool of award monies for themselves, how convenient.

Look, I can understand it if the managers were instrumental in creating something useful and lasting, and I don't mean taking credit for work done or created by the subordinates, which is what the majority of managers/directors etc. tend to do. There wasn't a director that I recalled that was not guilty of this practice, just take a look at their resumes. Show that resume to some of the subordinates and I guarantee they'll be in side busting hysterics.

Understand, even when I was written up for an award by public works to my department in the Design Division, that award never materialized for the caissons I designed, drafted up and managed each of the multitudes of twenty shops to produce, I did it all. Unlike the typical NAVSSES directors that phonies up a resume that they were instrumental in getting this and that project completed, and it's all hidden via resume technical hoodoo verbiage. I've seen some of their resumes and they all suck, filled with phony achievements. If these so called phony supervisors, managers and the director were truly honest, they would publish exactly why they received such very high salaries and awards and stop hiding them, which sounds so snake in the grass sneaky.

I know that if a local school official received a $7000.00 check, there would be an article in the local newspapers about it. So why doesn't the Navy do the same, after-all it's the taxpayers' money isn't it? Stop the looting and lies happening at NAVSSES now! It's the public money, and such huge outrageous awards should be made public and published in the newspapers. To publish such award and salary facts on the Intranet is not good enough, since the Military deliberately uses tactics, which hide such facts under a jungle of files and folder links with obscure titles. If there is such a link, it should be one easy to find link, with a title such as The Navy's Most Recent Awards, I mean Phony Awards.

Public servants that so much as had a favor done for something as little as a couple of hundred bucks have been fired and ridiculed in the newspapers. But at NAVSSES – well you know, it's military secrecy.

MANAGERS TAKE CREDIT

Basically, we all know that the subordinates' do all the research and the tough jobs, but it is the managers who receive the special awards if there is any coming. But fear not, if he like's you, the manager will make sure that he will mention your name for a pittance of some of the award. You don't have to know your job; the manager just has to like you. He'll try not to award anything to the mechanical savvy experts, because they receive satisfaction from knowing that they were assigned to the project, and that everything worked perfectly. The manager only seems to put in awards for the dumb people to ensure that they will advance to become the next supervisor, because frankly, the manager can't trust the award winning dummies alone on a ship to do the right thing on a piece of the ships components.

As a manager, he just has to sit back and ping his subordinates for a ridiculous status reports of their projects. Oh, and make sure that they don't clock out five minutes early, never mind that you might have arrived close to two hours before start time. Yep, that was I for the 39 years that I worked at the Navy Shipyard, I always left home a little after 4:00am. Did I get paid for all that extra hour and half time, of course not? Trust me, we had plenty of anal-retentive over-paid managers that would set up traps to catch anyone leaving 5 minutes early. Never mind that many of the employees could spend what seemed like hours every morning B.S.ing about sports or whatever every morning, or that they would leave the base for breakfast and lunch somewhere downtown, and return to work an hour and half later verses the half-hour allotted for lunch and none for breakfast. When did leaving the premise during working hours for breakfast at a remote site become the norm? Boy, people going and coming that easy sure makes for some questionable security issues.

So basically, NAVSSES it seems, rewards those who arrive at the start time and the late starters over the very early arrivers. You see early people, by arriving early, take care of all of those things people do in morning like take a dump, make coffee, and BS with friends, and by starting time, 6:00am, they are working. Whereas, the people that arrive just before starting time, or the latecomers, tend do all those things on company time. That time could run anywhere from four hours to as much as six hours of wasted time, if you include time spent smoking outside and taking long lunches. And yet from what I've seen, if you were to review the records of which class were often promoted and or lavished with awards, you'll find that they are predominately the time abusers. Doubt me? I dare you pull the leave records and compare them against the monetary award records.

The following are some of the reasons for why some of the upper managers refused to investigate, or question why one supervisor was putting himself in for so much ridiculous overtime. Much of it had to do with the person higher up looking away, because in a way, there was a guilt feeling for having won the promotion. So in other words, if I were to compete against another supervisor for the GS-14 managerial position and I won, I might let the loser feel better about himself, by allowing that other supervisor to make it up in phony overtime and traveling to nice places, carte blanc. I know for a fact about the phony overtimes because remember, I came in an hour and half before everyone else did in the morning. And every Monday morning I could see just who put in for overtime on the weekend. And without missing a beat, almost every weekend this one supervisor put in that he worked, no less than four hours. At fifty-two weeks in a year of overtime that's a hefty pay raise wouldn't you say. And they say that subordinates need supervising.
Directing, managing – I think not. Not any one of the upper management stopped to question the excessive overtime the supervisors were putting themselves in for. But, if I needed to work overtime which I rarely did, I needed a damn good reason, followed up the next day by, "So can I see what you did last night?" And if I was on travel, I was expected to provide them with a travel report of the people I met, the job, what was resolved, times of arrival and departure, and on and on in what amounted to a two page report.

Buying the Managers House:
By the way, it was a known fact, so I was told, that in my department one of my ex supervisor had purchased the manager's home in Delaware County, Philadelphia, prior to receiving his promotion to a GS-13 supervisory

position. I'll bet the Navy wasn't aware of that. What chance did the rest of us have against such collusion and deceit, for that same position? And this same supervisor was the same person putting himself in for overtime just about every weekend.

By the way, before this supervisor came to work in our section many of us had been in the department some ten plus years, more like sixteen years. Here I was doing what I considered an outstanding job and dressing as sharp as possible, and an outsider is selected to supervise our section. This guy knew nothing about our section except for the basics. He often came dressed to work in a pumpkin orange T-shirt. What kind of supervisor dresses like a kid on the street or dresses like some guy that resembles a cartoon character from the comics, The Far Side? He even wore T-shirts with wide horizontal strips, which is a no, no for a heavyset person, so much for my nice expensive professional white shirts and ties. I should have shopped at Cow Town for one of those rodeo clown outfits. Maybe, that was where I made my mistake.

And yet, the Navy felt that this person with little experience about our section and dressed in an orange T-shirt was the man to lead us. A clown set the standard. It wasn't long before this same supervisor was demoted or moved laterally from his supervisory position, but he was still able to keep his pay status. The demoted ex-super was reluctant to talk about it, suffice to tell us that he was assigned to do some other tasks. Who would have complained about that move with such a high salary? He had less work to do and makes the same amount of money – nice. What can I say? The guy overall was a nice guy, but why him as a supervisor? What about anyone else in my section, if not me? I knew more about our program than an outsider. This guy was an outsider. Just because two previous supervisors messed up our section, doesn't mean that we had anything to do with our funding going down. I didn't pick the incompetent jerks.

DICK'S TRAVELING CHARADE

One of my other supervisors, before Mr. Pumpkin Orange T-shirt supervisor came along, was Dick Willy. He was an ex-Navy Chief promoted to a managerial position without much experience in the field himself — unless you accept his time spent in the Navy as experience. Part of being a manager for NAVSSES, was to present oneself in Washington D.C. to promote our department. That was so that the supervisor could do a soft shoe for the Big Leagues in Washington, to justify the funding for our projects in our division. Well, just to give the reader a taste of Dick's incompetence, I'll mention a couple of scenarios we caught him at. One happened, when I was in Washington D.C. along with a fellow worker, Leo. We took the earliest train in the morning to Washington D.C. from Philadelphia. It left around 7:00am. Upon arriving at the train station in Washington, Leo and I boarded the subway train to Crystal City. Crystal City is where the big NAVSEA league fellows work, and the two of us were there to do business with some of our sponsors. I found a seat on the subway train and waited to get off at the sixth stop. In the mix of riders were two teenage Black boys both of them were dressed in scruffy soiled tank top T-shirts. The two started showing off with loud obscenities while hanging from the overhead handrails. Dressed in tank tops, their orange colored stalactite filled armpits were a nasty site for the rest of us riders to have witnessed, not to mention the ape like antics. I could see that the well dressed professional Black men and women seated across from me, wanted to jump up and smack the shit out of these two boys for showing Blacks in a negative light. I know it had nothing to do with NAVSSES, but I felt I had to mention these guys since it relates to one of my travels to NAVSEA. There's more like this Black incident.

We got off the subway, and Leo and I dropped off some manuals at the various NAVSEA departments and met with some of the officials to discuss some of projects. Leo went where he had to go, and I performed my errands. On the elevator going down, I encountered another two young Black boys, which appeared to be recent school graduates, wearing what I regard as the retarded looking hanging down pants. One of them was leaning on the wall to my left near the elevator's floor buttons. The other was standing near the back wall. So I entered and walked to my right as the door closed behind me. I turned to the boy closest to the buttons and said, "Second floor please."

"What—you think I am your personal elevator boy?" he said. The other black guy laughed and they both slapped each other's hands in a stupid dance routine giggling. "Slap me five."

I briefly shut my eyes, looked away, and walked over to the buttons. I pushed the second floor button. Those brats have no idea of how they just stereotyped their own kind, attitude, stupid attitude, and looser attitudes. Will it affect the way I see some black Americans in the future?

So what does that have to do with Dick Willy? Nothing, other than to show Blacks how they portray themselves in public, and to show them what Bill Cosby was trying say about Black kids today. Leo and I left Washington on the 11:30am train to return to Philly. So basically, Leo and I were in and out of the place in short a time, everything was completed before lunchtime. Prior to boarding, we stopped to pick up some lunch at a Chinese food court, to take with us on the train. We found a seat on the train, and low and behold shortly after as we were seated waiting to leave the Washington train station, here comes, Dick Willy, our manager. I saw him walk past my window to my left and board on the same car that Leo and I were seated in.

"Hi, Fellas!" he said as he walked by us. I surmise that he didn't expect to run into us in Washington.

Leo looked at me and couldn't believe it either. What was Dick doing in Washington getting on the 11:00am return train? He couldn't have met with anyone in Washington or dropped off any confidential paperwork. As soon as we got back to Philly, I asked our secretary what time our manager left Philly for Washington. She indicated he took the 9:30am train. Just as I thought - Dick took the train to Washington and immediately returned, just so he could put in for travel expenses and overtime. What a crook. Maybe, he had some business there, but I truly doubt it. Dick was promoted to a managerial position, and as such he was responsible for getting funding for our division. But instead, Dick was using his train rides to Washington just to get out of the office for the day. In the end, our department gradually withered into insignificance. I wonder why? Read on…

One of our managing technical representatives in San Diego said the same thing about Dick Willy's visits. Gorky our head rep in charge of the installs out there, at about the same time said, that Dick would arrive at his field office and ask to be ushered around one of the docked Navy ships. Gorky said that he would walk Dick around the main deck of one of the ships, and according to our field rep, Dick did not seem to care to go below deck to inspect or checkout some of our mechanical projects. You would expect that a manager if he's on travel and on one of the ships would spend some time investigating our work or whatever. Dick would instead get off the ship and leave the shipyard where the ship was docked. From what I was told, he would then go visiting relatives in San Diego. Upon returning to Philly, Dick would file for travel expenses and overtime - how convenient. Gorky wasn't the only field rep who told us stories about the do-nothing Dick Willy manager; there were other field reps as well who reported on his incompetence.

Yes, there were others like Dick who falsified up travel orders for monetary gain, and there were others like Kenny. Here was a GS-13 who prided himself on telling us that didn't have to pay back some travel funds, simply by writing the Travel Department a letter explaining that he couldn't pay it back because enough time had pasted, and it would cause him financial difficulty. Travel dropped the request for the payback. Here was a Supervisor making a fabulous salary ripping off the travel department, and to top that insult at the time, this guy owned roughly seven property rentals in South Jersey. From what he told us, I understood that he was clever enough to do some research into government documents about paying back monies due, and found the clause he was looking for. Creative moneymaking – I think so?

If any of us felt that the upper management would have intervened and done something about it, I can assure you that I would have been the first to complain about such corruptions. But since we all seem to understand that managers like Dick Willy would never be removed, his ability to retaliate was real. So it was best to just forget about it until now – this book.

ABOUT DICK

Dick Willy had this bad habit every mornings of walking away in the middle of a conversation exactly like the rude ex-supervisor, Rotty, who moved to the Platform office. "So what did you do over the weekend?" As I started to tell him about my weekend, Dick interrupted me. "Say - Good morning Kerry! Guess where I was yesterday?" And he would walk away like another jackass supervisor not interested in anything I had to say.

I call supervisors like Dick, jackasses because a jackass walks away from one grassy patch to another grassy patch. Many of the supervisors and managers only cared about themselves, typical egocentrics. We were just the fodder for their next promotions. When I saw managers like him, it was as if they came around to brag; "Hey everyone, look at me, I'm getting paid this huge salary just for showing up for work, isn't this great. I love coming to work. I can travel wherever I want and put in for all the over time I want, and look here, no one monitors my huge phone bills. I talk and you just listen. I can take any training courses I want, and I can deny my subordinates, any courses that they might want to take. "If you want something from me – just ask me to pull down my pants for a clear shot your ass. Oh, and make sure I get your status report before you leave today."

More about Dick:
Dick Willy, the manager with the stick up his butt look from the way he walked, also had another bad habit of insulting anyone in the office he didn't like. He did that by calling them into his office for some tongue lashing insults about their body odor, dress code, and such. If he didn't like your cologne, he would tell you it was offensive. I was taken aback when he did it to me. We had just come back from a meeting in Washington D.C. I had heard about his insulting mannerisms, so when he pulled it on me I said, "You know it's not me. You need to stop rooting through your cat's litter box for your deodorant. Sorry - I meant your candy bars because you keep talking crap." He never tried it again on me. Manager or not, I wasn't going to take his insults. If I was

wearing offensive cologne or whatever, I'm sure that some of the women I was dating at the time would have said something, including my close co-workers, and I had many of them.

In a way, his comment that I smelled bad at the conference had me wonder if maybe I had a problem. It's not something we like to admit, some of us do have strong body odor. I know that one of my Indian friends from when I worked in the Design Division at the shipyard had a strong Currie smell about him. I noticed that it was very prevalent when he offered me a ride in his car. The vehicle reeked like I was trapped in a decorative tin can of Currie and garlic. Per a talk radio station one day, I heard that Black's think Caucasians smell like wet dogs. Well for me, Blacks smell like spoiled lunchmeat smothered in vanilla coconut with a twist of orange rind. So where was I? Oh yes, I was picking my nose and I had fingered this huge bugger when I was called into Dick's office. After hearing his insulting remark, I flicked my sticky bugger straight at his face. It stuck to his left cheek like a mole. Well, maybe it didn't go anything like that, but that's how I would have replayed it, if it were possible.

On that day that I went to Washington with Dick Willy, we went to go over some of my projects with our sponsors at NAVSEA. I put on one of my best suits, and I wore my tan trench overcoat since it was still cold outdoors. And then to have Dick insult me later in his office was too much. What can I say other than to demonstrate; that what the Navy deems fit to be managers are often a joke. Me smell offensive? I was one of the few in my section who had no problems attracting friends over to my cubical to discuss all sorts of stuff, from working projects to them visiting me throughout the day for some friendly comradely, or to exchange home repair ideas and such. I'm sure if I had an odor problem, one of my many friends would have said something long before stick up his butt Dickey said anything.

Personally, I believe Dick Willy was jealous of some of us, especially me, because we outshined him at the many face-to-face conferences that we had in Washington. Yeah, Dick would come along, and say nothing at these meetings just so he could say that he was in Washington.

And as for body odor, I know for a fact that some of the guys actually thought I wore too much cologne in the office. For Dick to bring himself back up to our level, he had to lower us down to his repulsive snake in the grass personality. What better way to do that than with a degrading insult of your competitors? Actually, snakes wouldn't accept him in their reptile phylum. I could tell Dick too was trying to keep me down, because he had no college education himself. Dick was damn lucky for having been promoted to fill in as manager. Sadly, he really didn't do much to help our department and there were many in my section that could vouch for that. By the way there was one other jackass supervisor that made stupid remarks to his people after some meeting that went on in Washington. This guy would insult the person posture or they way one of guys placed his hands during the meeting. Nothing about how good the meeting went or what was covered, it was as if the supervisor wasn't listening but watching his people's posture, as if they were at some dog show.

While I was working for NAVSSES, we had a few elderly fellows that were either of German or Russian decent. I don't know what it is with the ethnic class, but these guys rarely changed their clothing. Many of them wore that same dingy food stained sweater year after year. Ear and nose hairs grew like artist paintbrushes. I can recall that when one of them finally retired, they had to use gloves to pick up the guys filthy computer keyboard. The keyboard looked like a garage grease monkey had handled it. Someone mentioned that they had to hit the keyboard with a bat to hold it still long enough for them to unplug it. Did the system/managers ever tell these guys they should do something about hygiene? I think not – they weren't competitive for promotions, but were still classified as engineers. Smelly ones if you ask me.

Before I leave writing about body odor there was other incident that I had with a supervisor from the Design Division. I detail his story in my other book, Mother's Chicken House. This supervisor actually stuck his nose to my shirt; sniffing it like a dog his name was Mike. The last I saw of him was as a contractor working for NAVSSES. We were in the Persian Gulf at the time riding one of the AGF class ships. Temperature outside was 115 degrees and 140 in the engine room. Needless to say, he couldn't smell anything on me, and he went about doing whatever. But I never forgot that embarrassment and hence I write about it, to get the crud off of my skin.

This same Mike, I'm leaving out his last name, put in one of his recently hired engineers for an outstanding award after we returned from the long twenty plus days at sea in the Persian Gulf. Now this was during the Monson season, and as you know many of the ships crew are going to get seasick. The young newly hired engineer that received the outstanding was sick in his bunk, ten out of the twenty plus days that we were at sea. It was oblivious that the management was trying to promote the engineers as quickly as possible, without them having earned their strips.

I not only completed all of my assignments on the AGF tracing out the air conditioning piping, I did the young engineer's work too. And yet, he was put in for an award while a supervisor sniffing out my shirt was my reward. Read the details in my other book. There's more to the story and very interesting. Moving on...

I'm not asking for a disproportionate number of awards and promotions go to just the technicians, but fair is fair, and what has been going on is not fair. When NAVSSES hands out awards to newly hired engineers just out of school while ignoring the existing professionals (Technicians or Engineers) – a fog of distrust is created under such disgraceful promotional practices.

When I transferred from the shop to a desk job in the Design Division of the shipyard, I attended many of the retirement parties and social events. I suppose you could say that I was some how hoping that besides the after hours schooling I was taking, plus the after work socializing might get me noticed and thereby promoted. Boy was I wasting my time. Guys like Rotty, Dick Willy, and one other supervisor like red headed Kenuts would play the "I don't see you game," at these social events. By that, I mean - whenever I tried socializing with them on some subject at one of these parties, they would pretend to be interested in what I had to say, but quickly looked away if someone of equal or high ranking importance entered their line of sight. I felt like I was talking to someone looking up at some aircraft-flying overhead. They were just a bunch of ugly rude phony supervisors and managers, who were just interested in them selves. They just wanted bodies at the parties to make whomever was retiring look that much more important.

Some of the retirement parties I attended were pathetic considering the many dedicated and long years of service some of the retirement guys put in. A simple lunch, some going away words and that was it. I felt bad for some of the guys leaving after so many years of dedicated work, so I wasn't going to stand still. At some of the future retirement parties that I attended, I would spend as much as $100.00 of my own monies to buy them a nice going away gift. I labeled the special gifts from the department. Many of the retirees spent their last eight years or so giving up all hopes of landing a promotion, after concluding that they stood little chance under a corrupt promotional and award system. I stopped putting in for promotions two years before I retired. That's how dishonest I felt my supervisors and managers, and basically the organization was. The place had the reputations of managers getting together not so much for the betterment of the organization, but to find creative ways of keeping the technicians down, and if not, they did it by blatantly stating so on the announcements. Technicians need not apply.

Technicians are like another tool. And to manage properly it helps to have people that disagree.

Two months before Dick Willy was to retire, his most expensive laptop computer disappeared. These were brand new laptops the Navy purchased for our division. At the time, laptops were just coming into being and expensive. Ours laptops were so-so with limited ability, more like a glorified pocket calculator with a couple of games. But Dick Willy's unit had the best of everything. How convenient. What a nice retirement award. I don't care what anyone else thinks. No one had a laptop disappear considering the fact that our laptops were out in the open. His unit was in his personal manager's office with a locked door – go figure? Say what you want. I know, I would have appreciated having a brand new laptop when I retired verses a template plague with my years of service spelled out, fit to place inside my fireplace. What I just mentioned about Willy's laptop disappearance is my opinion of where I believe the laptop is. With limited abilities running Windows 95, it's a very useless laptop today - but for its' day…

A SOMEWHAT ADMIRABLE SUPERVISOR

I only had one fairly nice supervisor at NAVSSES; I'll call him Flanks. This guy was good enough to provide his employee a token gift each Christmas. Not that anyone cared to receive a gift for Christmas, but at least he showed some interest in his people, in his halfhearted attempts to be a team player. The only thing I can fault him on was for not doing enough for us regarding outside seminars we wanted to take, and for not writing a letter to promote me to engineering equivalent. I had more than enough core engineer courses to qualify including a four-year apprenticeship, but no one, not even this nice guy supervisor had the balls to challenge the organization or to write a simple letter. I suppose, if I were promoted to their level I would be too much of a challenger competing against the same person, as I mentioned earlier. Initially, his excuse for not writing the letter was that he was recently promoted himself, and that he would look into it eventually. It never happened.

What can I say – thanks for nothing? In a way, Flanks was somewhat understanding, but as a supervisor, he failed miserable, especially when it came to seeking funds for our section… And as an engineer, well - I've never known him to do any of that. As a matter of fact when computer memory sticks came into being, Flanks foolishly ordered portable zip drives for everyone. Two of us in the office had already been using the sticks for a year and a half; we could see that zip drives were becoming useless. The brand new zip boxes that he bought for each of us remained unopened, and I turned mine in when I retired. Now for a supervisor that was supposed to be knowledgeable on up to the latest stuff, what can I say?

Not only could my memory stick hold five times what the zip drive could, it was a lot more convenient and easy to use. I don't know, but ever since I can remember I pretty much subscribed to all sorts of electrical, science and mechanical magazines. I never stopped learning, and when computers came into existence I eventually started a business doing websites for private customers.

Dick Willy another supervisor did have them review all of my college courses. Personnel came back with a report that mentioned that I just required one more course. They also indicated that if the management wanted they could rate me as an engineer, but it was up to him. Dick never wrote the letter. I have long argued, that the personnel department was not giving me credit for the other management courses that I had taken in college or my four-year apprenticeship at the shipyard. Those management and accounting courses I had, although they were not engineering courses, they made up more than enough qualifying credits as electives. Plus, I had more than my share of time served in the engineering trade, which could have served for course equivalents, but no one in any of my departments had the balls to file the papers on my behalf. The Navy is not the place to be, to be all that you can be.

There was more to my anger to the way NAVSSES picks and chooses who it wants to promote or give out awards to. It had to do with a correspondence school named LaSalle University that was located in Louisiana. I had learned about the school from an ad in one of the US Air magazines, and when I heard ads about this same college from a reputable talk radio station, WHYY, I felt that this was my answer to finally receiving my engineering degree. After all, if my supervisors weren't going to put me in based on all my subjects already taken, I felt that I could get it from this La Salle college. The ad said the college was accredited in Washington and the radio ad said the same thing. What could I lose?

So I applied and as usual they reviewed my courses and came up with an additional list of courses that I should take. There might have been about eight of them from what I recalled, so I paid roughly $3000.00 and completed the required courses. I received my engineering degree and I applied for membership with the national engineering associations and was accepted. When I showed my supervisor my engineering degree he congratulated me, and said he would look into putting me in. Personnel later came back with a statement that indicated that La Salle University from Louisiana was not an accredited college. What the fuck?

Needless to say, I investigated myself, and I discovered that in a way, what is accredited in one area may not be accredited in another and so on. In other words, a college is not going to give you one of their degrees unless you pay so much for it. Which explains why when you transfer courses from one college to another college, they won't accept all of your transfers least they lose money. After all that and more waste of my money and personal time studying for nothing, what was I to think of the place where I worked? I should also indicate that the majority of the colleges are a scam too.

As long as a person is rated satisfactory during a specific period, the Navy gives them credit for time served in their specific engineering field of business. It didn't matter that the Navy was dealing with engineers in Washington D.C. that didn't know what a basic knife switch was? All the Navy was concerned about was that the person had a piece of paper. I had designed solid-state circuits to fuel aircraft on Navy carriers, and I've written five technical manuals and so much more for goodness sakes.

The big wheels in the office would want you to believe that by attending the after hours parties, funerals and such that you could enhance your chances of being promoted. What a load of crap that was. They just wanted us to be there to make them selves' look more important. The smart ones saw the writing and stopped attending the retirement parties and such. Those still attending the after hours retirement parties were like sheep, too dumb to understand that they were being fooled into following a goat into a slaughterhouse. In India they have a name for it, which I can't recall. But over there, you can hire extras to attend your wedding or business seminar to make the celebrity appear more important.

I also heard from fellow workers after I retired, that my ex-manager retired in October 2008, and that none of the office subordinates attended his going away dinner. The only people there were the contractors of course and fellow big wigs.

DICK LOUDMOUTH AND MANAGER GLEASON

We had one other guy that was named Dick, but he wasn't a supervisor or manager. Like his name, he too was a dick you could say. What is it with guys named Dick? Are they all assholes or is it just - me? He came to work in our department from the warehouse section. This Dick had a very bad habit of blasting his telephone speakers for all of us to hear in the office, from one cubical all the way to the far wall. It was as if he wanted everyone in the place to know that he was important, and to prove it, he made sure his speaker was set to maximum volume. Hence, I'll refer to him as Dick Loudmouth.

Even when he spoke on the phone, Dick Loudmouth was extremely loud like a black person in an all black ghetto neighborhood or at a movie theater blabbering for all to hear. Sorry Black people but you know you're guilty. We had a Russian guy that did the same thing, but when he had to talk to one of his Russian friends over the phone, his voice was hardly audible. "Hey look everyone, I'm on the phone! Hey everyone I'm important!" It got even worst when Dick's doctor told him that his prostrate was cancerous. The whole office department of some 50 people or more had to hear the specifics of how his doctor fingered his butt in detail. It was sounding like his prostrate doctor had shoved his hand in far enough to play with Dick's testicles like a puppet. The only mistake his doctor made was not reaching in far enough to extract Dick's voice box. Dick by the way was an ex-chief from the Navy too. Maybe, that had something to do with his offbeat office mannerisms.

When you leave the military, can you ex-Navy chiefs stop talking like Black people in the movies? You sound so retarded talking so loud for all to hear. I don't know, maybe, all that engine room noise morphs the Navy chiefs into speaking loud to be heard. It could be that the constant engine room noise destroyed their hearing.

When I mentioned Dick's loudness to my over paid manger, his response was, "Did you try to talking to him about it"?

"Yeah, right me talk to the ex-chief. I see you have no experience with ex-Navy chiefs." That was his job as manager. Like I said, NAVSSES pays these guys to be managers but they can't even make the place a friendly place to work. They have to ask us to do their dirty work. Anyway, shortly after I complained about the loud mouth, he lowered his voice but only for a week or so. Actually, his loudness was also mentioned to my ex-supervisor, and he too saw nothing wrong with the way the guy was constantly slamming down his phone, and for talking ridiculously loud. And it wasn't like the guy couldn't lower his voice, because when he wanted to talk about personal stuff besides his prostrate, he did.

I came very close to taping the loud mouth's phone conversations, and then replaying them whenever he tried to talk over his speakerphone. Can you imagine what it would sound like if all of us in the place had our speakerphone on loud everyday? What a jackass.

I might also mention a really evil manager like Gleason. Just mention the gay manager, and just about everyone at NAVSSES who knew Gleason would tell you that they knew whom you're talking about. Just the way he dressed and flung his arms around said, gay. Working for Gleason, I had an incident where I faxed a message to a fellow worker in Washington to chop. In the message, I mistakenly wrote the word CONFIDENTIAL. The same fellow worker named, Dick Loudmouth, picked up a copy of the receipt from the fax machine and noticed the word CONFIDENTIAL on it. Now Dick Loudmouth knew that it was a partial of my message, but decided to be the hero and gave my partial copy receipt of the message to Gleason my newly elected manager at the time.

I was called into Gleason's office and asked about the fax. Gleason seated facing me with his legs crossed as if he was holding back a fart. Gleason, noting there was nothing at all confidential on the message still went ahead and wrote me up in a letter of reprimand. What better way to look like a manager in his new promotion?

The way it all happened is that all of us in the office, basically copied pre-issued messages to make sure we got the naval distribution format right. Recall that I said the Platform Office should have been responsible for distribution list? Anyway, the Navy had a rigid way messages were to be sent, and we all had to follow this template. It just so happened, that I used a message with the word, "Confidential," written in the template. I should have used one that said Administrative message. Anyway, after finding a partial copy of my draft message in the fax machine, Dick Loudmouth took it and handed my rough draft to Gleason, instead of coming to me regarding the silly mistake.

The majority of the fax receipts were usually trashed daily. It was a shame to see such a pile of wasted paper. Only one woman in the office required a receipt of her faxes. Actually, she really didn't require a copy, but she wanted proof of all her work. Every fax sent printed out a portion of the message sent as a receipt of what was just faxed over the phone line. I would reset the machine every so often to save paper, but some asshole would reset it after me to print out a receipt copy. I thought that when computers came on the scene, we were supposed to save paper or become a paperless business. After that incident with Gleason writing me up, I just included a blank page in front of all my faxes. That way the receipt only copied and printed a blank page. Others in the office caught on to my way of faxing and started doing the same thing.

So, the copy of my message with nothing confidential written on it except for the word CONFIDENTIAL went from Dick Loudmouth to Gleason, our acting manager at the time. Gleason called me to his office and I sat down. We discussed the message mishap, and I thought that that was it. It wasn't, Gleason issued a letter of reprimand. He put a copy of that letter in my files to remain there for three years. What a sphincter mud head for doing that, after I had 30 plus years of excellent servicing. It was a simple mistake – for God sakes. Why couldn't he have just given me a warning? And get this, that same manager told me that he was going to do everything in his power to get me fired. Can you imagine that? This same big time jerk that was still working closely with the director after I retired. Abuse of power - I think so?

This is one of many such insults the Navy places on the hard workers. I can't imagine what other subordinates had to deal with in their departments.

Anyway, there is nothing that the Navy keeps secret that isn't freely available from existing commercial ship builders, the Intranet and books. The ship schedules are readily available for all Navy personnel loved ones to follow their whereabouts. Anything that had to be sent by message could be sent a lot more efficient via emails. But, the Navy continues to insist it has something secret to keep, so they continue to use the old complex asinine message transmission system. The existing system reminds me of the Tarzan movies where the native beats on a hollow tree trunks to send messages. Messages that the Navy deemed secret are at best retarded and laughable. I could only surmise they were marked as such by clowns moonlighting as mummers for the annual Philly Mummers parade. It's only one of many such ways that the Navy attempts to appear important to the Joe Blow public.

For the managers working for the Navy to think for one second, that I or anyone else who was not insulted and hurt via a letter of reprimands for such ridiculous incidents, this book is my answer, and it could have been much worst. A letter of reprimand is comparable to calling someone a witch, once your marked your career/promotions are fucked. Some individuals had endured so much pain and become desensitized that a visit to the dentist for a root canal would have felt like a vacation. So why should I enjoy coming to work anymore or do an honest job anymore? Read-on...

Recall, that I mentioned having to move from one cubical to another or from one building to another. Well, whenever we had to change buildings, confidential and top secret papers and or confidential technical manuals were discarded into several huge dumpsters for trash. No one was ever assigned to ensure the so-called secret technical manuals or message papers were disposed of properly. Often the dumpsters were left unattended for weeks and months while the building was cleaned out. I saw top secret CDs, military tapes, and floppies in the mix of trash. So for my spineless Captain to go along with what Gleason wrote about me demonstrates, that when the Navy wants to play the vindictive card, they can and do. And they do so without concern of the consequences.

Part of being able to travel and board Navy ships without much challenge was a list of NAVSSES employees, listing birth dates, place of birth, GS rate and social security numbers. This list was sent out to all Navy surface vessels with little help to any of us wanting to board a ship say in Norfolk. We still needed a message or some other confirmation. But the list of names was a start to help reduce clearance messages whenever someone from NAVSSES was to visit one of the ships for whatever. Not only did all the ships get a copy of this personal employee information, we all got a copy too. So what does this mean? It means that not a single person was ever told to return such list during employment, or asked to return it before anyone of these people retired. Guess where your name is presently used in that list?

Remember the Postal workers? Maybe, they had an agenda too. One has to wonder. There was a study done by congress that determined that better than 98% of what the military deemed secret was in fact not so confidential after all. There was absolutely nothing at all that I can ever recall in my thirty plus years that was secret in any of the message that I saw marked CONFIDENTIAL or SECRET in my department. Much of what was identified as secret was done so by the Navy in my opinion to make the department appear more important than it really was. Much like the loud mouth Russian or like Dick Loudmouth when they spoke very load to make sure everyone heard him.

By the way, there was another bad habit Dick Loudmouth had, and that is that he would discus his project in minuet detail, talking from start time in the morning until it was time to go, talking about the same stupid project. I pity the contractors that had to listen to him everyday. Just having to hear him talk about the ridiculous, like making sure that they had a flat blade screwdriver and hardhats before they boarded the ship, made me feel like shoving a series of firecrackers in my ear canals and lighting them off. It was pure torture, day after day, of dumb stupid ass loudmouthed people and managers with primordial bean counting intelligence, which I had to deal with at NAVSSES.

Funny, when I took notice of SURFACE WAREFARE OPERATIONS/ CNO AVAILABILITY SCHEDULE FY papers that were left in the remote printer one day, I mentioned it to Mr. Loudmouth who had forgotten about them. You see, the remote printer was located just outside of his cubical, and how he forgot that they were there, sitting out in the open for a couple of days, one has to question why. I was good enough to tell him before dropping off the papers on the manager desk to get Loudmouth written up. I mentioned to Mr. Loudmouth that we had Muslim Janitors working in our area emptying our waste baskets, and that it would be easy for one of them to get their hands on the papers. "YOU'RE A RACISTS, THAT'S WHAT YOU ARE - YOU"RE A RACIST!" That was his response. It was obvious that he knew that I had caught him, making a more grievous mistake than the one he tried to accuse me of, which mine was nothing more than a message with the word Confidential on it. Mr. Loudmouth ex-chief had left a complex spreadsheet of Navy ship schedules in the fax machine for days.

Psychologist would no doubt label Loudmouth a Megalomaniac = A psychopathological condition characterized by delusional fantasies of wealth, power, or omnipotence. And a Narcissistic= arrogant, windbag, loudmouth, cocky, selfish, conceited, domineering, stingy and self-centered.

By the way Mr. Loudmouth was promoted two months after I retired, and it was only because he was in charge of an expensive air conditioning project. A project that could have been easily handled by the shipyards verses costing millions more via NAVSSES. So here is a guy that yells over the phone, like the department is selling fish at the Italian fish open market, with his belly button showing for that street bum look, too cheap to buy the proper size shirt. A very heavyset person in a child size, white T-shirt with horizontal broad green strips does not make for a professional person to look up to. Or maybe, just maybe, that is what NAVSSES is looking for, just like the woman that goes shopping in her pajamas and flip-flops. Oh my – I guess that was my mistake. I forgot to dress sloppy like a vagabond. Yes, Mr. Loudmouth was a very heavyset man, and he wore a T-shirt so small that a third of his belly would bulge out. Promoted, how laughable is that? A fine example of professionalism - I suppose for NAVSSES.

So here was a guy that definitely had sensitive papers left in the printer for a couple of days, and I get written up for having a piece of paper with the word confidential written on it. My single piece of paper was in the fax for ten minutes at most. Go Figure? The Muslims janitors by the way, came over recently from one of the very small African nations, located on the West coast of Africa close to Morocco. Morocco by the way, has been producing a crap load of Islamic terrorist as witnessed by the train bombing in Spain and many of the roadside bomb experts in Iraq and Afghanistan come from there too.

Mr. Loudmouth was also awarded a Presidential award, which like I said comes with having been selected to manage an expensive project. So while the rest of us were handling thirty-four projects with tons of nit picking problems and complexities, this one project obnoxious guy gets all the attention and a cake to boot. When I designed two 400 horsepower fire-fighting caissons for the SLEP program – I got shit. Onward…

On another occasion, Gleason also tried to write me up for missing a gathering to discuss the stupid. The meeting was to be held at a remote site some four-miles away off base. Every once in a great while, our department at NAVSSES held a group meeting off site - as they referred to it, to exchange ideas and such. Basically, it was just a waste of good taxpayer's money. The department was trying to use up the previous fiscal years funds to ensure that each year that they would receive the same or more funding the following year. This form of accounting waste went on year after year. None of us could blow the whistle about such waste; least we lose our job from retaliation, demotion, and such. The way the off site meeting worked, was that one of the managers would rent out a conference room at some plush hotel like at the Holiday Inn in Philadelphia. Some crummy lecturer was hired to speak on some really dumb moronic subject, and then our group was to discuss the subject matter. I attended these loser gatherings years after year, and I always felt we were just wasting our time and money that could have been better spent.

Then one year, I decided to remain in the office to catch up on some work. Actually, I still had a slight fear of crossing over the bridge. It's a long story regarding anxiety from over working – you have to read my other book to understand what happened. Anyway, Gleason, my manager wrote me up for not attending. I complained to the Captain that Gleason's letter of reprimand was not justified. I presented an email to the Captain from Gleason himself, in it he told our department that nothing was accomplished at the meeting, and that the time could have been better spent. Slam-dunk. I shoved it up Gleason's ass. The Captain agreed and had him retract his letter. I also explained that there wasn't a need to go off site for a conference when our huge conference rooms on base were all empty, and we had several empty conference rooms and buildings ever since the Shipyard closed. I suppose, had I put in for sick leave, Gleason would have had nothing to say. In other words the Navy teaches you to cheat.

While I'm on the subject of the Big Jerk Manager, Gleason, I should mention the over-paid Director's secretary, often labeled assistant to justify her huge salary. I know I mentioned her before, so what? Anyway, here was this over-paid woman that one day, or I should say, on several occasion E-mailed a list to everyone at NAVSSES their names, date of birth and Social Security Numbers. The E-mail was in reference to some questionnaire about taking one of those childish security questionnaires. Anyway, it wasn't until I mentioned it to Manager Gleason that it stopped. And yet, this woman wasn't written up or whatever. As a matter of fact, you couldn't even ask this menial clerk, or I should say recalcitrant paper shuffler, a simple question like I did once.

It seems one day that she had sent us an E-mail with an attachment to look at and respond. I opened her E-mail, read her brief letter, but there was no attachment to look at, let alone open it. The over-paid assistant forgot to include the attachment. So, I E-mailed her back asking her for the attachment. Well, you can imagine, the woman freaked out with a response as if I was harassing her. She had sent a copy of her complaint E-mail to the director and my supervisor as if to say, "How dare you ask me for something!"

Flanks, my supervisor at the time, looked over the E-mail, and he couldn't find anything wrong with what I asked her in it. He told me to just stay away from her, and he indicated that she has some issues. So, there you go. A director's assistant, I mean a belligerent whatever, that can't even answer my E-mail intelligently is paid over 90,000. I call it big time, waste fraud and abuse, by the director and the Captain who have been well aware of this woman's shortcomings. If they need to promote women the assistant is long over due to be replaced.

There was one other woman with a very nasty mannerism, and she worked in the clearance badge issuing office located close the main entrance. It seems that quite a few people from NAVSSES that knew her had had at one time, a bad encounter with her. I can recall one time arriving at the badge office around ten minutes to one, long after lunchtime was over at twelve-thirty. So I waited quietly outside of he office with the window shades pulled down and the glass window closed. At around eighteen after one, I got up from my seat and walked over to the shade-closed window. Through the shades I could barely see her inside making out with what looked like one of guys from the shop. They were hugging and such, so I tapped on the window to get some service. A bit of shuffling inside and the shade went up and the window opened.

"Don't you ever tap on this window, blah, blah, blah"!

"I was sent here to get my security badge renewed."

Needless to say years later, I heard from others that our new Captain, a woman, dressed in civilian clothes at the time had a similar encounter with the recalcitrant bitchy badge lady. The woman was moved to another office and replaced, but she didn't lose her job.

TRAINING

If I put in a request at NAVSSES to take a special seminar off base, I was often denied. But, it was ok for the management to waste huge sums of money for stupid senseless meetings off base. Never was anything ever accomplished at these wasteful meetings, and there isn't a single person that was at them that would contradict what I am saying.

Training seminars year after year, that were offered by our department were all totally useless. I called them, "Waste my time courses." Many of them were mandatory. Most of them were on site and others were given just off base. The typical courses were, creative writing, dealing with people, or some program on how to use a very basic computer program. The only ones benefiting from these loser courses were the private institutes that were offering the courses. The Navy in turn could turn around and claim that they were training and offering courses that were helping the personnel or something like that. Actually, anyone that ever attended one of these courses often dozed off during the seminar, or made up an excuse to leave early.

After repeated denials to attend the seminars that I wanted to take instead of the garbage stuff the Navy was offering, I sent an ultimatum to my Supervisor. Basically, I emailed him a letter that spelled out favoritism. I told him I was going to contact waste fraud and abuse. I asked him to explain how one of the supervisors in another section could travel to Florida for a seminar, and I couldn't sign up for a cheap course down town? The other guy, a supervisor, had all expenses paid to Disney World Florida. He had a hotel, travel, car rental and more for a basic supervisory course. When I investigated the course that he took in Florida, I found out that the same exact supervisory course was being offered at roughly the same time in Philly. The course I wanted would have only cost $200.00 verses the thousands that they spent for the other guy to travel to Florida. I later found out that he took his family with him to Florida – how nice. This was just one, of many such favoritism, the Navy managers and Supervisors were perpetrating. And then they can't figure out why some people go postal or retired in disgust.

The supervisor I mentioned that got paid to take training courses in Florida was I Claudius. He had some Italian background, and when he spoke he sounded like he just came off the boat from the old country. Even his emails were difficult to understand. Maybe, if I had a box of spaghettis, I could drop them like pickup sticks and come up with some ancient Tuscan code for deciphering his emails. Whenever I saw the guy, he reminded me of some guy behind a counter in an apron making pizzas. He just had that look about him.

On a couple of occasions Claudius was called to make a brief speech at one of our conference meetings held in the auditorium. Maybe, he was asked to say something to the group to justify his GS-13 rate. His speech amounted to telling our new comers, the field reps, where the bathrooms and the snack bar were located. God forbid if one of the visitors should roam aimlessly about our halls in search of the restrooms. During his speeches, he would interject one of his most stupid jokes. They were so badly told that the audience often had to complete the punch line. A supervisor, GS-13 – Oh yeah – sure, tell me again that this guy was of deserving such a rate. Paper or not, this guy was certainly over rated.

And while I'm on the subject of training courses, I learned early on, that although the Navy claims that they would reimburse an employee for taking college courses, the truth is that all the managers I knew would find some reason to deny the reimbursement. They did that by claiming that the course wasn't relative to the person's job. In other words, because I was a technician, I couldn't' take engineering courses. I could only take technical courses, such as the silly technical writing crap. It was obvious that once again, the higher ups were doing all that they could to eliminate competition by keeping their people down. The manager was keeping his people in a box, and as they say, not all that you can be.

Shortly after, our manager Dick Willy retired, we were assigned an anal retentive supervisor named Walnut. Walnut had a bad habit of writing down ever nuance we conveyed to him. If I told him about something I did at home during some conversation, like a problem I might have had with the car, he would take note of it and jot it down. Come time for our quarterly evaluations, Walnut would use that information he gathered to use against us.

I learned quickly not to tell him anything. A team player and caring person he was not.

Walnut by the way was reprimanded for throwing out my mail. I wouldn't have known he was doing it had I not glanced at the waste bucket, on one of my returns from the men's room. I saw my name on one of the letters. Walnut was throwing away just about anything that wasn't important to his people. There were electrical and mechanical design magazines, flyers, and just about anything you can imagine that's considered business or industrial literature of mine in the wastebasket.

It was Dick Willy who was acting manager at the time; I mentioned to him that I had been waiting for one of the letters that I found in the trash. The letter contained important component dimensions vital to one of my projects. Walnut was briefly notified to stop it, but as you can see that when a person is in the managerial/supervisory position does something of this gravity, the Navy scratches cat litter over it. But should a subordinate do the same – well that person can expect a letter of reprimand in his folder.

Later when Walnut wasn't promoted to a managerial position, pissed, he opted to move to another department. Initially I suppose he thought he was hurting our department by leaving.

With Walnut's office cubical left vacant except for some paperwork about our projects and such, some of us were able discover his sinister record keeping mannerisms. Walnut wrote like a typewriter using very small lettering; size 6 fonts, when he wrote. It was as if he was attempting to hide the fact that he was a sneak. "Maybe, if I write real small they won't be so offended if they ever find out? My writing is so tiny it can't possibly be considered harmful." Well - you can imagine the detailed daily records he kept on us found their way to the dumpsters. Walnut finding the records missing left a message scrawled on a sheet of paper in the same drawer. It said, "If I EVER CATCH THE PERSON THAT WENT THROUGH MY STUFF." Someone added another sheet to it that said, "Ooooooh - I'm so scared of someone still living at home with his Mommy." What a dick.

At Walnut's new job, someone from his section told me that the management pulled down his pants and shoved a broomstick up his ass with splinters on it – meaning they forced him to take a job in Pascagoula. You need a major flight to get there from Philly. There, he had to spend x-amount of time overseeing a project that lasted for a few years. He was allowed to return home periodically for whatever. Most of us don't mind having to travel now and then for short periods, but to have to be away from home for months or years are another ugly matter. Working under such extreme distant conditioned must have had affected Walnut's hair. When I saw him three years later after leaving our section, he had lost much of it. Everything on top was missing or too thin to notice. At that point, he could have volunteered as a Franciscan Monk and fit right in.

Walnut didn't exactly treat us bad, but there's just something about trusting someone that keeps exhaustive records on his people. At the one end of the spectrum, he would evaluate me as being very confident in handling my projects, and he even mentioned that I had some of the most difficult projects. But come evaluation time, Walnut would put someone else in for an outstanding award.

Receiving an outstanding rating meant you qualified for a fairly large monetary award. In one instance, the award or recognition was given to a woman. I won't mention her name. She was a recent college graduate. What could she possible have excelled in to qualify for the divisions outstanding awards? I on the other hand was rated satisfactory. I with all my experiences and years of service was rated sat. Maybe, he did it because he was told to do so.

At the time, the Navy was scrambling to promote women to show the Navy was in compliance with some marching orders from Washington – discrimination stuff you know, quotas. It didn't matter if the woman qualified for the promotions – just promote them up quickly the supervisors and managers were told/ordered, no matter the qualifications.

What was I to think, when NAVSSES was promoting mechanics with a basic high school education and women to fill past mismanagement decision-making positions? And when the Navy was basically ordered to promote more women in the business, they promoted secretaries instead of hiring women from the outside that had engineering or technical degrees. Time and time again, they promoted the less qualified. Of course there were exceptions, but few if any. It wasn't that I cared about the secretary women getting promoted over me. I understood that the Navy had marching orders to give them priority like the Military did for the Blacks in the past. That's where the Blacks were given an extra 10 points on a test just for being Black. I just felt it was wrong to promote secretaries into technical positions over some girl that was far more qualified, from putting in the time at some university or she had experience from working in the mechanical shops. It wasn't fair to the women that had made the effort to get educated into such fields. A secretary made no such effort.

To fill some of those women positions, some of the contractors had their own secretaries apply and get the high paying jobs. From speaking to one of the person's that did the interviews and or evaluations of their resumes, he told me that they were told that if the girl had in her resume that she did this or that, to give her points or credit for it. Give them points, even if the interviewer felt or knew that there was no way this woman did any of this stuff she was alleging to have done. You see the contractors knew exactly what to put in the woman's resume to get the woman hired by NAVSSES. Fair, I think not when compared to the women who bothered to take technical school courses. Plus when the Navy was ordered to promote more women, it didn't advertise for them. It just promoted what they had available in-house. Thankfully, one of them wasn't a janitor.

Finally, I had seen enough and I decided to file a grievance for the unfair rating I was given. It was the only way to make a change hopefully. It didn't, but here is some of the stuff I complained about to the captain in my grievance. For one, I mentioned that one of my most difficult projects was given to the woman that received the award in my section. Three months later, that same project was thrown back on my lap. Absolutely nothing was done on it, no paper work, no installs - nothing. And yet in the write up for the woman's award, the supervisor said, "She set an example."

She "Set an example!" – Give me a break? The woman for one, and I am not the only one that said this about her, had a bad habit, while seated, of crossing her legs in a short skirt while facing some of the guys. What do mean by that? Well, it means that whenever I had to see her for something in her cubical, she would turn towards me with her legs crossed in her chair and her feet tucked under on her chair. I could easily see up her skirt, and it was obvious she was trying to play her flirting game on me. Fluttering her eyes while she talked to me was a cheap shot; she must have thought I didn't notice. But what could I say? What is it with some girls? They think that because the splayed legs in the air worked for the actress and singer, Barbara Strisand, in one of her prisoner movies that it must work on all the guys.

Like many individuals the Navy wanted to promote, NAVSSES falsified outstanding awards to pad the candidate's records; thereby ensuring whom they wanted would get promoted. The open legs woman was one such person along with many other individuals that got promoted using such phony tactics.

Guys like Rotty and some others I knew from the shop were moved up the ladder, or promoted not so much because of their mechanical abilities, or because they bettered themselves from taking after work courses at some college. They were promoted by knowing someone that could put in a good word for them. If you knew someone that could lay your resume on the supervisor's desk, you were pretty much guaranteed to get the job. And that is exactly what was going on at the shipyard in the design division and at NAVSSES.

Me like a fool, spent thousands of my own money taking college courses hoping to get promoted. But it wasn't to be. My leave record was impeccable, and I was always one of the first guys in at work. I even volunteered for the toughest jobs because I enjoyed the challenges – but?

The fluttering-eyes woman did eventually get promoted all the way up to a managerial position. Who would have guessed it - yeah? And I must say she seemed to be doing a good job at it. I even told her one-day that I was impressed with one of the presentations that she gave at the auditorium. It seems that all the managers I ever had were required to do one of those one-time presentations in front of our department. It kind of ensured to everyone that they were qualified. Of course they always had a few months to prepare their speeches along with some power point presentation. And like just about all the dog and pony shows, there was nothing said at these phony gatherings that we didn't already know.

All of the presentations could have been divulged via some e-mail, thus saving wasted time. The presentations were awfully boring. I was half tempted to buy a set of glasses with the open eyeballs, so I could sit in the back and catch some Z's while they blabbered away. Oh, by the way, they did pay for the woman to spend some time in Washington to see how things operated up there. Making contacts, getting to understand where the funding originates and so on, were some of the things she learned. It may have been two or three months she was there - maybe longer. I guess the time spent in Washington helped her get promoted too, but how come none of us were asked for that kind of training? Well, you know why.

There was one other woman that got promoted without any experience for the position. She moved all the way up to the director's position. While we were all socializing during one of the holidays, I recall her telling a group of us in the machinery alteration department, of how little she qualified for the position. She said, "When I was promoted to the job I knew nothing about it, and I'm still learning." So there you have it folks right from the horses mouth. Boy was that a bunch of crap. All that time I was signing up for various training courses, attending classes after work and doing everything to look competent, and yet here was proof that the Navy was promoting the most incompetent. She was just another person at the right place at the right time.

Whenever I had to list all my experiences on the government forms they gave us for an opening, there was never enough space to put down all my work and educational history. Oh sure, somewhere on the form it tells you to use another piece of paper if you have to, but I just know the people working in the Navy personnel department weren't even bothering to look at the second page of qualifications. Heck, if they did, I wouldn't have received notices that I didn't qualify. Those losers already had someone picked for the promotions time and time again.

As supervisors and managers they were responsible for holding meetings and making presentations to the people in Washington. But hardly any of them did. This caused much of our organization to gradually dwindle to a handful of employees. I could see the writing on the wall. Over time, I was prevented from going to Washington, just so that the inexperience punk out of college could appear more important to our contacts in Washington. And as expected, within a short period, the little whippersnapper became our supervisor. Like a bunch of juvenile ostriches, the newly hired graduates would gather into tight nit clutches during lunch break, while the more mature and experienced passed by disgusted at what they were witnessing. A bunch of snot-nose kids with no past experiences were gradually taking over the place. Too old to complain, many of the seasoned masters remained silent while waiting for enough time in to retire. Such were some of the managerial abuses perpetrated that I witnessed while working for the Navy at NAVSSES. But, I was different and this book is my way at speaking up for such abuses and injustices.

By The way, I don't know of anyone who really wanted to retire voluntarily. Most of them did so because they were being harassed via a slew of constant underhanded managerial tactics.

RETALIATION

Retaliation at NAVSSES comes in subtle ways to where the employees being retaliated against can not file a retaliation report because; it goes something like this; if you do, you can expect excess traveling to trivial jobs far from home, you'll get constantly monitoring where you go and when you return, you'll receive lowered awards or none at all, lowered ratings, extra useless paperwork, request for daily status reports, denied extras like cell phones, denied the latest computer and or training seminars, nick picking your messages and or the useless status reports, repeated rewriting of your contracts even after you wrote them exactly the way the manager spelled them out, and so on and so on...

My last manager made the point of jumping into my booth un-expectantly several time in an attempt to try to catch me doing something illegal on the Intranet. In another retaliation attempt, he made the comment in an Email that my report on a limited space spreadsheet status report was of seventh-grade level. And yet, everyone in my organization who saw my spreadsheet found nothing wrong with it. The manager was the first to ever make a negative statement, on any of performance ratings that stated that the field reps were having difficulty in getting me to respond to my emails. He did the same with another technician in our group, and we were the only two in my section that did not receive an award for that period.

Meanwhile the recently hired into our group young woman recently out of college was rating with a special award attached letter. By the way, I contacted the field reps and they all denied ever saying anything about how I responded to my emails. Most of my contacts with the field reps were always over the phone. Retaliation comes in all forms, most are too subtle for the top management to notice, or they care not to notice least they have to rectify the situations. The Director signs off on the ratings and the people rated have no recourse to correct or defend themselves. Going Postal – I think so, if not in the near future, it's in the making from the hurt such despicable managers place on the hard working personnel, which is sanctioned by the director and the Captain. Stop the excuse that an attack was unforeseen before one does occur. The Captain and director is very much responsible if something does occur for allowing managers to abuse subordinates and doing nothing to resolve the inequality or promotions, training, awards, and so on. When the ship goes down, investigators will be questioning the Captain, not the employees.

I can't tell you of how many times I have witnessed snot-nosed young hires, promoted to supervisory positions, say insulting comments to some of the best hardworking contractors during project status meetings. Most of the comments were degrading and uncalled for, but what do you expect when young adults are given free rein to push and degrade the moral of veterans and the experienced? Professionalism and respect – I think not. Potential future trouble – you can bet on it.

FUDGING OVERTIME

I had other similar supervisors and managers that abused overtime. The most common way that they abused overtime was to consistently put in for it every weekend. I was usually the first person to arrive every morning around 4:30am. And every Monday morning I would see my supervisors name on the sign in sheet, for a minimum of four hours of overtime that he supposedly did either on Saturday or Sunday. I can understand putting in for overtime now and then, but to consistently see his name in for overtime every weekend and weekdays has to raise a red flag. This guy was taking home an extra $400.00 minimum every week for years.

Now we all know that people in general, when left all alone for four hours or more in a work environment, they tend to fudge about how many overtime hours they really put in. What makes a supervisor any more trust worthy than a commoner? Some guys even knew how to circumvent the system on the computers and sneak in a few hours here and there without anybody noticing.

Nuts - when I was on travel inspecting some system on a Navy ship, I always felt guilty asking for overtime. I don't know what it was, but it just felt icky calling up my boss to tell him I'll be working late. Somehow, I didn't think he would believe me. Working late on a Navy ship after just about everyone left the ship in the evening, was like working on an abandoned ship. Outside of ventilation sounds and a pump discharging, not much was happening onboard. So, when I left a message on my bosses phone to put me in for overtime, it sounded like I was calling from my hotel room. Maybe, I should have prerecorded some clanking sounds, an engine starting up, and so on. Then I could play it back while I left a message, kind of like running water while urinating at a public urinal. It just felt better hearing the water in the background. With background noises, I could pretend to not hear my boss, if he happens to pick up the phone to challenge my overtime request. "I have to go now; they're starting up the engines, bye."

And it wasn't just the overtime the Navy was making me feel guilty to claim, the reams of paperwork just to recoup monies that I spent to buy incidental parts I needed to complete the job, from a hardware store, wasn't worth the effort. But others didn't seem to be phased spending a couple of hours filling out paperwork for something like sixty bucks worth of refunds. Even when I had training at some remote location within my state of New Jersey or in Philadelphia, I never put in for the measly gas mileage refund. It wasn't worth the crap that NAVSSES required getting it. I had too many projects that had priority. But for others – no problem, they were going to get those ten bucks worth of gas, no matter how much paperwork was in order.

We also had a couple of women in the office, which were abusing the overtime, weekend after weekend. It wasn't until after I complained to my supervisor, that it was getting ridiculous, that something was done to curb much of the overtime abuse. One of these women would spend much of her time on the phone all day B S-ing with relatives around the United States.

When I first transferred from the shipyard to NAVSSES, I couldn't believe what I was hearing this woman discuss over the phone. The woman in the next office to mine was calling a Kmart outlet in Ohio for information regarding $3.00 sneakers. She wanted to know, when they would be on sale in her Philadelphia area. This was when phone calls were somewhat expensive and no one was allowed to call home unless there was an emergency.

There was this other woman wasting similar time over the phone. She would discuss dog shows with other contestants, or she would talk with potential buyers about her pedigreed pups for sale. Both of these women would discuss such garbage for hours, and none of the supervisors said anything about it. Come the weekend, and the dog lady was sure to put in for her four to six hours of overtime to get her job done – go figure. And don't tell me that her supervisor wasn't aware of her phony overtime requests, because the two of them were coming in together.

Phone calls:
In the past whenever my supervisor reviewed the monthly phone bill, out of state phone calls were not challenged because they appeared as legitimate business calls, hence the dog lady making out of state calls about her dogs.

But should I call my Mom in New Jersey to see if she was ok was taboo. The supervisor had a list of our home phone numbers and knew if we were making personal calls. But for a person living in Philly close to the base, that person could talk all day with relatives, while the employees that lived in New Jersey or Delaware were tagged, because those calls were charged as long distance. Back then, long distance phone calls could add up to hundreds or thousands of dollars. Today it's a different matter, anyone can call unlimited around the United States for a fix small fee. But can the Navy explain why some managers, supervisors and newly hired college kids have phone tabs that look something like $3000/month? And guys like me were not even allowed to even own a cell phone, even when I was on travel. And to think, I had all that excellent work and leave record - Shameful of the director and my managers.

Paydays:

Payday was another waste of the taxpayers' money. On payday, a line would often form at a local bank while the employees were on the clock, including some that were belligerently shopping for groceries while on the clock. The cover-up was to have someone in the office, tell others that they were on a ship doing some inspection or such work, or they were to say, that the person was in conference in another remote department – distant building. Nothing was ever said about that. Employee cashing in their checks at some local bank felt even more secure when cell phones came into existence.

SECRETARIES

Many of the secretaries that I had the pleasure of working with were another huge black hole of incompetence that the Navy imposed on us. And I'm not the only one that complained about many of the secretaries' limited skills. For instance, there wasn't a letter or a message that I didn't write and type myself prior to handing it to my secretary to proof read and pass on. Why have secretaries, if I have to do all the typing? God forbid, if one of my letters had a grammar mistake or misspelling.

And don't even mention the way some of them dressed – so unprofessional. It got to the point where not even the secretaries cared how they dressed. Some of them would come to work in Atlantic City beach slippers, smacking their flip-flops as they walked about our department. It was always distracting having to hear the loud smacks along with Dick Loudmouth yelling over the phone, while I was trying to concentrate on something. Can a guy do that, come to work yelling while walking around in flip flips and a Speedo, perhaps? Only at NAVSSES.

So where was I? Oh yes - our funky looking secretary, I had to hide to one side behind her partition just to drop off one of my paperwork in her in basket. This bitchy person didn't have any couth in telling me that something was wrong with my paper, like a job order, or date. She would have to shout it out for all to hear. "HEY EVERYBODY LUEDER MADE A MISTAKE; THIS IS THE WRONG JOB ORDER!" It was the only job order my supervisor gave me. And yet, year after year the secretaries were given an award for outstanding work that many of us felt was more like garbage than anything else.

The managers even requested donations from all of us for the great job the girls were doing on secretary's day. What could I say? We all put in something for the collection least we look like cheapskates. I had to reside to the fact that my donation was probable going to feed some strange wildlife. I just made it easier for myself to give, like shifting gears. Remember, if you don't play along, the supervisor will tweak that annual performance rating…

So just give her the five bucks on secretary's day, two bucks is too cheap. And these were secretaries making what secretaries on the outside would kill to be making, and there was an annual bonus to boot. I'll probable get some of the secretaries to mail me back my five bucks in an attempt to insult me, but you can only insult if I receive five bucks for each year that I worked at NAVSSES.

And before any of you secretaries consider refunding, ask yourself, what did you really ever type for me, or any one of the subordinates for that matter. All of us did our own travel requests, messages and purchase orders. Secretaries if anything did work for the manager, and he should be the one taking her out for secretaries day etc.

Now, had I been working in the private industry I wouldn't have cared to donate, even knowing that the secretary did zilch for me, because in the private world secretaries don't make that much.

MESSAGES

Why the hell should I have to learn how to write a Naval message, when that is suppose to be the secretaries job. All I should have to do is provide her with the details, and it should be up to her to layout the proper Navy format. They had so many changes to the message writing format that all of us in the office had to keep a stack of Navy message as templates, just to make sure we got them right. We should not have had to do that. And you guessed it - there was always something wrong on the messages we wrote. It could be a code that changes, a project leader that changed, or a ship that was decommissioned. That is the secretary's job or the message center to keep up with those changes, and not the people doing the technical work. Time and time again, messages with the most minor mistakes were rejected causing delays, wasted paper, and frustrations in field, and all because of an idiotic rigid Naval messaging system.

And forget about getting a message out on time. There were always some idiot supervisors or manager that had to ejaculate his own thoughts or wording on my message, so as to demonstrate his dominate position in the kingdom of the living dead brains. I believe just before I started working for the Navy, they did away with the red wax blob imprinted with some ship insignia before a message could be sent via pigeons. On some of the buildings you could still see some of the original messenger pigeons hanging around.

Even after I got everything right on a message, the right codes, the right needs to know commands, etc. the message still had to pass a battery of chops up the ladder. You guessed it again. There was always some ape up the ladder, which felt that the way he scratched down his grunts made more sense than mine. So, not only did I have to rewrite my simple clearance message, I had to hand carried it back up the same chain of commands. "Not that same message again!" the secretary would bark back in disgust. And if it wasn't the secretaries' job to write messages, what is wrong with the Platform department writing them besides just shuffling the messages around while making outrageous salaries? Sure why not the Platform office writing the messages? After all, the technical codes have to deal with technical subject matter, and the Platform is all about the shuffling of ship locations and messages, etc.

BILLY GOAT

Billy Goat was another one of those evil anal-retentive managers. He had a bad habit of pacing around the office jotting down notes about each employee. Surprisingly he was stupid enough to email his peek-a-boo findings to everyone. In the email, he documented moment-by-moment if a person was sipping coffee to nibbling on a snack. The report was embarrassing to everyone in his department. That report was forwarded to the Captain, by one of his subordinates, and as expected nothing happened. As a matter of fact, Billy Goat continued to be the big jerk that he was.

In another one of his strange cases, Billy Goat wrote up a fellow worker for telling another worker on the second floor that he could take one of the filing cabinets marked for trash. We had just relocated from one building to another, and the old gray trashy looking cabinet with stickers all over it was clearly labeled for the dumpster. No one stole anything. Another person was trying to put the filing cabinet to good use in another department upstairs.

But that wasn't the way Billy Goat saw it. This ape viewed it as – no one had asked his permission to reuse the cabinet. Can you imagine - a high level engineer has to ask permission to recycle a used file cabinet, verses the cleaning crew hauling the unit out to the dumpster? A simple talk between the two wasn't sufficient for this manager. Oh no, he was determined to write him up, and up he did.

Now we all know, that personalities come in a variety of colors, which makes assessing a person's ability for violence a bit challenging. There was no doubt that Billy should have been demoted long ago, due to the numerous complaints filed against him. The interesting factor about Bill's antics for punishing someone severely for minor infractions and I can't even call them offenses, was his vile behavior as a manager seemed to be overlooked by several of the Captains.

As a manager, Billy Goat was responsible for soliciting funding for the department. But instead being the spineless person he was, Billy spent much of his time reviewing the employees' daily sign-in sheet. He was more concerned about people signing in 5 minutes late or leaving 5 minutes early. I always came into work an hour and a half before start time, but that didn't matter to Billy Goat. He was going to make sure, I signed out anytime after my quitting time and not a second sooner.

Five minutes late or early meant more to Billy than all the B.S. going on all day long at the office. Employees running outside 14 times a day for a smoke were not questioned. In that gaggle mass of people were those individuals that didn't smoke. These nonsmokers felt that if the smokers could get all this free time standing outside, they too should be entitled to the same. So the non-smokers would spend just as much time outdoors socializing with the smokers.

Lunch hour is supposed to be one half hour long, but many employees were leaving the base to eat at some restaurant in Philadelphia. Often these out of base eaters returned from lunch after an hour and a half or more. Not to mention, that these same employees didn't break for lunch at 12:00, but at 11:30. Nothing was ever said. Football and baseball game discussions could go on for hours with Billy in the mist. He would add his sports commentary as if to tell participants that this kind of waste of time at work was ok. But if I catch you leaving five minutes early... And in the men's room some of the idiots would leave the water blasting into a coffee cup while they were in taking a crap. All that water waste wasn't a concern to Billy.

For goodness sakes, if the Navy was so concerned about when people arrive and leave work, all they had to do was check the computer that allowed access to the secure building via a card reader?

Oops, I forgot they're engineers, maybe they forgot how to do that or forgot how to program the system to supply that sort of info.

It just goes to show you that useless managers like Billy, often amplify the more menial aspects of managing. In other words, if you were to ask a child to supervise a bunch of children, he would manage them by using a stick to keep them in line. The managing child looks to keeping his group corralled making sure no one wonders beyond the box that he has created for them. The last thing on the child's mind is how best to utilize all their brain power, or how is he going to feed them. Bill was like a child void of the crucial understandings of what it means to be a manager. The people he was dealing with were highly skilled workers and not a bunch of children, which needed to be told when they could start and stop work. One hundred and fifty thousand dollar salaries for such morons, are the people in charge of the NAVSSES nuts?

Billy, too stupid to be in Washington D.C. to get us funding, hid behind his incompetence by pretending to be a stern manager, by monitoring the employees working minutes. When Bill couldn't view what was on our desktop monitors, he would rest his nose over one of our partitions believing we didn't notice. I would have loved to have the metal trim in my cubical electrified with an ignition coil. It was easy to know he was there from his ghostly image on our monitor. The idiot one day jokingly made a comment that he would like to see mirrors placed above the employee's cubicles. You can imagine why.

And this is the funny part about this man; Billy was Catholic. He was one of the people selected in his church located in South Jersey to give out communion. He once asked one of two women twins we had working at NAVSSES as to why they never walked up to him for communion. One of the twins told me at work that she didn't want to tell him to his face, that he was a hypocrite and an evil person. Working close with the personnel office, the woman and her twin sister were both very much aware of Billy's nasty ways.

MOS

The Navy implemented a program to monitor work performance; another one of those useless tools that churn's out a three-dimensional pie chart. It was called (MOS) for short, Management Operating System. Albeit, the program has merit in some areas, but the Navy used it to the ridiculous extreme. By that I mean, everyone was ordered to input something every week for every hour they spent at work. If you were going to be off on one of the work weekdays, you were expected to enter the information that you would be away information too. And some bonehead employees initially thought this data collection system was a great program. They were inputting each and every email response, breaks, phone responses, meetings and such nonsense. The list could be as long as twenty entrees per day. Not too hard to do when there's funding for your projects. But when the war in the Middle East sucked up most of our funds, project came to a stand still - just about. Now what do you put into MOS? You guessed it, everyone started making up stuff. It was either that or you received a nasty email from the manager. Not a single person up the chain of command had enough sense to mention a simple fix. God forbid if some of the guys reported that they had nothing to do. And yet the Navy has tons of reserves that do just that. They report monthly or whatever and receive a check for showing up for roll call. Give me a break.

Many of us caught on to the programs faults. Some of us inputted entries that did not end until the end of the year. That way, we wouldn't have to fake something new everyday. The people monitoring the entry attempted to crack down on practice of yearly entries, but that didn't go too far. Most of us just thumbed our nose at the request and continued entering the same useless information.

So where was I going with MOS? Well for one, managers like anal-retentive Bill, he had a bad habit of reminding anyone that missed his MOS entry, not just that particular week that he missed it, but he also mentioned all other weeks that that person missed via emailing to everyone said person's mistakes in the department. It was as if Bill was out to make an example of the delinquent person. This is the same manager that hands out communion in church. Sounds to me like, he hasn't learned a thing about forgiveness of mistakes. Bill seems to enjoy slapping the other cheek as long as it isn't his own. Bill even sent out an email telling us that he was keeping a list of who misses an entry into MOS. He also indicated that he has a separate list for anyone that fails to supply a status report every week. How can you have status to report without funding to get any one of your projects moving? What a jerk.

Sadly, the Navy had no testicles to demote supervisors and managers; least they open themselves up to lawsuits. When someone in the managerial position did something wrong, the Navy would cover it up by dismissing it. But, should any non-managerial person commit the same infraction, a letter was put in their records or worse. The only thing missing at the office was a whipping post, you could say. The place became so strict that it was as if, they wanted supervisors that could insert a cannon plug in our skulls, hook it up to our computers, and build scaffolding around our head to keep our eyes secured and fixed on the computer monitor screen. And if you had to go potty, well the wastebasket was close by.

DOCTOR FRIEDMAN

NAVSSES is not production or services driven. NAVSSES is much more likely than a private company to sacrifice economic efficiency, in order to achieve individual management political goals. For the Navy to claim that it prefers individuals with no talents, and then molds them according to the Navy ways is a bunch of crap. That's not what the Navy wants, it's what your immediate supervisor wants out of you to make himself more superior, over all others below himself. The Navy wants to control the people's attitude while blanking out your creative abilities. Working at NAVSSES was comparable to a visit with Doctor Friedman, the father of the lobotomy surgery, employees become brain dead sports fans walking around with IVs and oxygen masks. And like the doctors in the past, NAVSSES cowers under a veil of immunity to criticism via a false pretense of effective and efficient operations. Say what? First of all you have to be producing something tangible and secondly it has to be worthy, neither of which is conducive of NAVSSES.

Pretzel sales, hoagies on Thursday and bake sales or whatever wrapped in used pie chart paper is about as creative as it gets at NAVSSES. Day after day, I counted down the days while feeling my creative abilities imprisoned by boneheaded managers, until I could retire to another realm of sights and sounds.

Does anyone know of another business that is so embroiled, with fund raising an internal convenient store operations, mixed with a sprinkling of sports gabbing socializing - because I would like to know about it?

Should the Navy try to justify NAVSSES smatterings of little private money making shops as fundraisers, then, may I suggest that all accounting be handled by a third party? Just two people running the candy soda show just don't seem fair for lots of reasons. For one, there's no telling how much is pocketed for personal monetary enhancements. Secondly, many of the people that cannot partake in parties held in the city of Philadelphia for various personal reasons, somehow, always lose out in benefiting from these galas. Not fair, wouldn't you say. I for one was cheated out of many of the Christmas parties, and no one reimbursed me some of the fund raising monies to use as I wish. Even a prepaid dinner card would have been nice.

But no, people like myself who couldn't make it to many of the holiday parties were and still are constantly being cheated out of the profits collected, profits which were meant to benefit everyone. What about the sick or those people on travel? And what about other religious sects that couldn't attend many of the parties funded from the fund raising?

One thing I noticed most often was that the people who benefited the most from these parties were the alcoholics. Yes, I said alcoholics, because they were always held at places where they served alcohol, and to surmise that much of those funds were not used for booze, you've got to be kidding. Look I can understand fund raising for a noble cause, but to raise money for parties? Come-on NAVSSES, are you management trying to say that $90,000 average employee salaries, isn't sufficient for the employees to pay for their questionable parties?

Is anyone at NAVSSES doing any serious work? Let see, starting late, begin worked after two to three hours to settle down, leave for an hour lunch, return and leave again to replenish candy and soda fund raising store, restock store, collect the money and sort the bills, and it's time to sign out it's the end of the day. Is this why my ex-manager and others like him were awarded $7000.00 bonus year after year. Please will someone at NAVSSES show the public, the work done for such outrageous squandering of the taxpayers money?

START AND STOP

Start and quitting time was another one of the most disgraceful mode of operations practiced by the Navy system at the organization where I worked. When the Navy allowed flextime that allowed us to start and stop work in increments of some set times. The Navy unperceivable was favoring the lazy people. At least that is the way I saw it, and I'll explain why. The earliest they would allow us to start was 6:00am, which meant that we could leave at 2:30pm or after putting in our 8 hours. I was always in work by something like 4:30 am. That meant I wasn't getting paid until 6:00am or an hour and a half later. So everyday I was putting in an additional hour or so, free for the Navy. Now for those people coming in late, and then let's say they put in an extra hour of overtime, got paid for it as overtime. Not fair. The management got so paranoid with my early start that they requested I forge my time coming in to after 5:00am. So after that personal threat order, I fudged in that I came in at 5:05am.

So, what's wrong with the late starter you might ask? Well, for one, early starters get all their stuff done before the actual time to begin work, while late guys bullshit the first two or three hours upon starting. Late starters run to the latrines right after their first coffee, discuss baseballs scores, and visit one another before even starting anything. Early people have their coffee; take a toilet dump, visit and what not, so they really put in full eight hours of work. And yet the Navy seeks to reward the latecomers over the early people. All I was asking for was to start work at 5:30 or just a half hour earlier. Year after year, whenever our union contract came up to renew the start time, the Navy was adamant at favoring the people that waste time bullshitting at work. Now, I'm sure some of the employees had legitimate excuses for not coming in early. But com-on, I know my truth speaks volumes and believe it or not, it was usually the late starters that seemed to get promoted most often. The ones that wasted the taxpayers' time were more likely to get promoted. Don't believe me — try taking a survey.

Working from Home:

In line with the core working hours was a request I made to my Captain requesting the possibility of us working from home. My argument per my email to him basically said, that there was absolutely nothing we did in the office that couldn't be performed from our homes. His answer was that it was up to my supervisor and manager to decide that issue. I fired back with a response that said that neither one of them would ever approve of such a suggestion, because it would undermine their own positions. Actually, it is terribly ridiculous to even have supervisory positions, since the majority of the workers are professionals with a history of satisfactory performances. The people that need monitoring are not so much the lower ranking personnel as much as it is the much higher-ranking individuals, such as the director and the captain.

The farther up the professional ladder one is, the more damages they can inflict on the system, because they have carte blanch pretty much on spending, decision making, promotions, and such. These guys can make million dollar mistakes, whereas the little guy might fake an hour here and there in overtime. Plus if the organization fails, the top managers should be made to step down, and not hang around like rotting fruit to spoil those around them like ours did.

Shortly after the 9/11 Muslim terrorists attacks, I sent another similar email to our Admiral, who seemed to enjoy sending us silly template letters about holiday concerns. And get this, he's an overpaid, say what? Anyway, my email requested that he investigate, as to why NAVSSES was fighting the written recommendation from the top that stated, that if the employees can do their job from home that they should be allowed to do so. In other words there was a letter sent from higher ups suggesting we be allowed to work from home – but nope. My letter to the Captain was a lengthy email message, but you decide...

In my email, I mentioned the many benefits of working from home which including a tremendous monetary saving. For starters insurance cost goes down, building rental cost goes down or away, maintenance goes down, utilities in the millions goes down and then there is security of the employees. What better way to protect government workers than to spread them across the tri-states? By placing most of us in one building, a terrorist can easily kill a slew of the government workers. And what about spreading diseases and viruses and the list can go on.

During such times with high fuel cost and pollution from everyone having to drive to work, NAVSSES is mentally locked into the past, by insisting that its employee must be there five days a week for forty hours, week after week. For NAVSSES to continue along such draconian decision-making is outrageous when the world is crying out to reduce the carbon footprint. It obvious since I retired in January 2008 that the management still doesn't get it, and why should they when it's not their money they're squandering.

Everything we did was either handled with a phone call or via an email. Can you say, "Outsourcing," because that is what the place is about? Just about everything from developing complex flow charts to hands on repair on a Navy vessel, were all done, by outsourcing the tasks? And don't even mention in-house meetings because every one of them was a waste of time. There was absolutely nothing said at the meetings that couldn't have been said in an email. Also the numbers of meetings were few and far between, which proves that the meetings at NAVSSES were filled with crap like information and boring. A person on death row would have begged for the death injection than have to endure senseless hours of nothingness meetings. And to think that we were ordered to attend them or risk discipline bordering on dismissal.

NAVSSES should have been labeled ending with an OS, instead of ES, OS meaning Navy Ship Systems Outsourcing. If you're going to outsource all the engineering work, how does the Navy justify so many engineers doing project managing? Project managing that any secretary can do, "Hello original manufacturer, say can you help me out with this component, that the Navy bought from your company?"

In this day and age of game playing there is no reason, why the Navy cannot come up with similar solutions to everyday Naval craft solutions and such. A virtual world of some specific system so that everyone within NAVSSES can review and study the problem in a team like atmosphere, is the way of the future to solving such complex problems. Instead, what you presently have is one or two people at the most, who might understand one system like a specific ships switchboards.

Wouldn't it be nice if more people were looking at the problem and coming up with solutions? In a virtual 3D world of complex machinery, solutions can be tested and verified. Teamwork with challenges, verses a sweatshop of managers constantly harping about a retarded message, which could have been resolved via a phone call or an email? Challenges like coming up with trousers with built in floatation bladders, ROV crafts, and what about a May-West with a salt to freshwater straw? These and a slew of other ideas could really wakeup the institution, which, frankly, is a huge embarrassment of potential talented people doing nothing that benefits no one.

Sometimes, being too close to a problem can cause the person to draw a blank, verses someone reviewing the problem from a distance. To ensure that those individuals who provided concrete solutions to some of the complex problems, a point system can be can be addressed next to that person's name. Receive so many points and you get a reward, this method stops the secrecy and mystique of who gets what and explains why, so that all can see. Trust me, even the funding dream catchers can be rated in a similar fashion. You know — the ones tasked to get funding.

Problem solving on complex equipment when properly executed, is setting your self up like a well-oiled company, whereby the manager stands away from the assembly line workers, far enough where he can oversee the whole plant. If the manager were on the assembly line, he would be too close to one particular function and lose what is occurring to the rest of the plant. And it's this closeness that often causes those responsible for one specific piece of equipment on a surface craft that makes them lose the big picture. A virtual 3D world of the problem would eliminate much of the horse with blinders problem solving, that presently exists at NAVSSES.

And by working from home, no longer does the Navy have to rely on a handful of people, which live within a reasonable driving distance to work. Talent can come from as far away as Montana and more.

FROM THE ADMIRAL

From the admiral, "Wow, you seem to have some issues but I'll look into it and get back," he responded in his email. He didn't, the jerk admiral just passed it on to some Captain, who sent me a copy of the same request letter to work from home, that I already had a copy of and knew all about it. I told the Admiral that we were packed like sardines into one major building, and we have no guards at the main gate anymore. You see our managers and some secretaries have to make $149,000 salaries, plus huge bonuses awards so that the Navy can no longer pay, to have some minimum wage guards check badges at the main gate anymore. And then I added with a title like Warfare Center why shouldn't the terrorist consider our place for a target? Anyone can easily drive in the Navy yard with a fuel truck and crash it through our building, what's to stop him. After all, just recently cruise ships were allowed to park to within two blocks of our building, so fueling trucks for the cruise ships were not considered suspicious.

What I was getting at was that, with no guards to check people entering the fenced in shipyard, our building with several thousand of us in it, were vulnerable to attack from terrorists. If the shipyard was turning over many of the existing abandoned building to the private sector to convert for commercial business, then all of the remaining people working for the Navy should be made to move to building 1000. Building 1000 was big, fairly new and secure with a tall secure fence around it. Unlike our building which could have been like any other building in open Philadelphia.

But no, the Navy instead scatters its people throughout the ex-shipyard into various buildings and within easy access to terrorist attacks in non-secured areas. A repeat of Timothy McVeigh's attack is a possibility with such easily accessible buildings. And should an attack occur, what does the widower get, some measly government insurance and a pension. Monday morning quarterbacking...just like the FBI that failed to have secured entrances to their satellite offices, stupid, stupid and stupid. Yeah, look into the FBI's records and there you'll find, that the FBI were so over confidant that no one bothered to have a sentry at one of their satellite offices. Some guy with an agenda simply walked into one of their office unopposed and shot up the place. And don't even mention the Green River Killer and how the FBI really screwed that investigation to the tune of some fifty women killed before Gary Ridgeway was arrested for the murders. NAVSSES is no different, it exist in an air of false security, all the while labeling itself, The Warfare Center, how lovely.

PROMOTION BENEFITS

Getting promoted to any of the managerial positioned seemed to open up all sorts of benefits. Unlimited overtime, unlimited phone usage, they could pretty much buy what ever they wanted for office supplies from a new laptop to the latest digital camera. They could apply for just about any training they wanted and travel to the best bases located at the best beaches. Managers could break for lunch and return whenever they wanted and so much more. The rest of us were seen as individuals that fit within a box, and whenever we did something outside of the box, meant that they were free to step on us. And step they did from making some of us go for extremely long durations away from home on some frivolous ship inspections, to denying us training and over time at will. And I'm not even going to go into abusing our annual ratings.

Management at the shipyard and at NAVSSES was structured into forcing the employees into boxes of conformances. I'm not sure where I heard it from that we all belonged in a box, but it's a concept that NAVSSES uses as a way to control the employees. The lower down the GS scale you were, the smaller the box they put you in. Get a promotion and the box they placed you in increased in size. Become a manager, and you sudden found yourself outside of the box to where you could stomp on all the other boxes at will.

Some of the employees were stomped on to the point that they feared peeking beyond their box's rim. Fear such as I mentioned earlier about surfing the Intranet. That box concept might not be so bad for military personnel, but it made no sense for individuals like me, which are creative free thinkers.

CREDIT CARDS

Issued Federal Military Credit Cards was another one of those big wasteful black holes the Military does wrong, especially the Navy, witness GAO reporting millions in suspect purchases 2008. I don't know of any business that freely hands out credit cards to its' employees, to use for travel without some form of controls. Let me explain. You see, with a free credit card some sinister employees are going to find creative ways to use it for personal stuff. And this is how easy it is to do. I give my card to a friend, and he in turn goes shopping with it. Back at work, I report a stolen credit card, and the Navy issues me another one. This can go on repeatedly until the losses amount to several thousand dollars to millions.

If you think that the enlisted men or that the low ranking individuals are doing this, think again. Much of the perpetrators is officers and well paid management office personnel.

In the end, the taxpayers' pays for the bungling credit card loses. When I tried to complain about it, I was threatened that if I didn't use my issued military card for travel, I would be disciplined and possibly dismissed. Collusion and kickbacks between the credit card company and some ex-naval person, I think so. In the end the taxpayer suffers, which explains another one of those outrageous military costs.

Absolutely, no one in the military or working for the military should require a special issue Navy credit card to travel. Everyone who works for the NAVY or any military institute makes a comfortable salary, and they should not require using a taxpayer's credit card. If their credit is bad - too bad, you're either fired, or you are required to get some counseling. Almost all travelers know exactly where they are going, and they setup their own reservations ahead of time, along with the hotel and the car rentals. I'm sure every one of the major hotels will gladly accept a credit card number over the phone, or via some computer confirmation method for payment of services received. With this method, the traveler does not require another stupid credit card that can easily disappear or be misused.

If you think these freely issued cards are not a problem check with the military, under freedom of information. The last time I looked, the losses to the taxpayers were several million dollars, heading for the hundreds of millions. And yet no one cares, because the average taxpayers assumes that because the credit card issued fiasco is a government sponsored program, they must be knowledgeable and trustworthy in what they are doing. Remember the big wigs at Enron or the housing failure?

GAO: Millions in suspect purchases, April 9, 2008. Funny the same week that I was writing about credit card fraud, I see this article in the local newspapers. So while I was being threatened dismissal if I did not use the government issued credit card, others were actually doing exactly what I had been saying. The article indicated cards were used for gambling, lingerie, Internet dating, paying for prostitutes and some two million were spent on adult toys that could not be accounted for. And to think, that the very people that threatened me to use the card were the same people, who were stealing from the public - Dicks. I was working amongst big time thieves, can you imagine? No wonder they wanted us to all use their credit cards. The more people using them, the more society begins to believe that they have to use them, and what better way for thieves to hide their activity.

It's kind of like the guy with a mole on his nose. It doesn't look right but after repeated encounters with such person, you get used to seeing the mole as it over time sports little hairs, to look like a palm tree. A handful of credit card thieves in a vast ocean of people seem trivial on the surface, until the taxpayers receive the bill.

Trust me, if every one of the government workers had to use their own credit cards for travel, you would see ridiculous expenses go way down, ASAP.

Travel waste:

Another big waste of taxpayers' monies was in reporting travel expenses. To report traveling expenses, we had to fill out reams of paperwork just to get back a measly $40.00 sometimes. Talk about a $300.00 hammer. There is absolutely no reason why some military travelers cannot be allotted x-amount of dollars for x-number of days travel – period. No paperwork required.

If the traveler wishes to sleep in his rent a car or a friend's house, that's his business. There exist plenty of information on historical travel expenses that the Navy should have no problem allocating a fixed fee per travel destination, etc.

But no – the military follows up with reams of paperwork that can at times end up costing more to process, than the total amount allotted for the travel. And why couldn't a single secretary do our travel order, and then file all our paperwork. On the outside in the industry, travel paperwork is a secretary's job. That's part of what the secretaries get hired for, aren't they? We should not have had to waste our time trying to learn how to file for travel orders and such. That reader - are your tax dollars being squandered for engineers doing a secretaries job. See what I mean about incompetent directors, managers, and captains – they don't give a damn, it's not their money. This and many other wasteful systems had to be said in the hopes, that someone up the ladder will do something about it. Plus it was part of my life, and my taxes – why else?

Pizza and More:

Pizza, hoagies and pretzels are the highlights every morning at NAVSSES, notifying everyone in the various departments, where they were being sold in the building that particular day. Fund raising, yeah sure, as if the highly paid people at NAVSSES couldn't afford the $5.00 or $15.00 to have a holiday party. And if that were not enough, several highly paid GS-12 & 13 individuals had setup complete cubicles to sell everything from candy to aspirins. They would purchase goods, off load them and sorted the goods all during working hours, remember the late arrivers.

All the while, the guy barely making a living in the lunchroom was being undermined by the satellite luncheonettes sprinkled about the command. NAVSSES management blind to what was going on with multiple convenience stores, was putting this poor handicap blind man, and the few minimum wage hires out of work, just like managerial brainiacs did with the house cleaners. House cleaners making minimum wages were put out of work, so that the NAVSSES could award its managers huge bonuses every year. Fair, I think not.

You would think that an institution as big as NAVSSES would be doing something to help out, the huge unemployment in and around the city of

Philadelphia. Jeepers – I should have opened my own Bass Fishing shop selling fishing poles, live worms and lures.

Lighting and Water:
Just about every morning when I arrived early around 4:45am, much of the building inside was lit up via incandescent floodlights. Even after I mentioned it our Mrs. Captain in 2006, nothing was ever done to cycle them off during the off hours, or to change them to energy efficient fluorescent bulbs per my suggestion. "Yeah that's a good idea, I'll look into it," she said. And why do all the multitudes of lights in the heads (water closets) have to remain on all night. See what I mean about a useless Captain and director? It's typical of many of the higher ups; they got their promotion, now it's time to sit back. I Got my metal, my promotion, my, my, my…and like the monkeys no hear, no speak and no see they wait to be told what to do next. Two years after I mentioned the lights and retired, the place still uses incandescent lighting.

Precious water waste is another issue with what's wrong with the way the Navy monitors the employees' usage. I can't name all the times, that I witnessed individuals running the hot water at full blast while taking their time shaving. We even had some individuals that thought nothing to leaving coffee pots and personal plastic lunch containers sit in the sink with water running over them while they took a dump or left the room for whatever. Boy - don't you wish you could be this wasteful with your water and lighting at home.

TROUBLE IN THE NAVY

I guess I should mention something about the Navy where I worked in Philly, and where I feel it is heading. I understand that they are attempting to do away with the technical employees and hire just engineers with huge egos. What a big mistake that would be for several reasons; for one the bulk of the work is repair work? What better person, to know how to fix a complex engine than a technical expert verses a bookworm? An ex-chief from the Navy understands the ships equipment better than some kid just out of college.

Secondly, when I was there during any of my 39 years, none of the engineers were performing engineering services. The situation is not going to change overnight. Sure, some of them might claim they were doing engineering, but much of the work was already designed and tested by the original manufacturer. Whenever an engineer at the shipyard didn't know how something worked or operated they would call up the manufacture for details on the product. Heck, a secretary could do that. Oops, I forgot that the Navy did promote secretaries all the way up to GS-12 position, and there was one that I know of that got his GS-14.

There was zilch engineering work at NAVSSES from what I saw, causing engineering abilities to atrophy. The Navy then replaced engineering with time management – labeling it engineering. You would think that we were scheduling a battleship to land on the planet Mars, from the entire nit picking useless data we had collected.

No – I believe the whole organization needs to be overhauled with better checks and balances. And I don't mean using existing personnel. That way, much of the salaries won't be spent on a bunch of feathered chiefs strutting about like peacocks, verses the true problem solving performers, the technicians. The techs were on the front line doing all the fighting. What I observed was a bunch of overpaid draftsmen working at the shipyard design division, and a bunch of overpaid managers working at Naval Surface Warfare Center in Philadelphia. Like I said, we had secretaries promoted to the same high rate of pay, because they could do the same work as an engineer. And if a secretary could be promoted to a technical GS 12 position, why was the Navy advertising constantly for engineers at a much higher pay scale?

I know that the title of the place is titled Engineering somewhere in there. But the fact is, rarely less than two percent at NAVSSES is truly engineering. There isn't a person at NAVSSES who can provide proof that calculus was ever part of one of their assignments. And if they did, it would fall in that less than two percent of people doing such work.

A true engineer was someone like my wife's father who worked for Acme food distributors. He was responsible for calculating all the stresses and strains, to various structural designs of Acme buildings and exterior signposts. I reviewed much of his work after he passed away, and I was very much impressed from his detailed records. In the 39 plus years that I had working for the Navy; I was never impressed by any of the engineering stuff I saw performed there. Some outside manufacturer or contractor had already done much of it. All our engineers had to do was to review someone else's work.

Often a pump was manufactured, but the Navy would insist on testing it again themselves, duplicating the same tests. This was nothing more than waste and more waste of the taxpayers' monies. Shock and vibration testing, give me a break. A handful of Arabs in a rubber boat proved just how reliable those shock and vibration tests were. And you know what? The Navy hasn't even considered that maybe one day, a Muslim nut job will scuba dive, a mine exactly where the Navy refuels in the Persian Gulf. A mine underwater can be set to go off remotely, Hello. "Ghee, we didn't see any rubber boat this time. Who could have foreseen that?"

Speaking about test facilities and NAVSSES, there really doesn't have to be a test facility at NAVSSES, because test facilities already exist in all the shipyards that build Navy ships. Can we stop the duplication of work? The test facility that does exist at NAVSSES is pretty much, like having a car's dashboard in your living room to test a new oil pressure gage, before installing the gage in your everyday vehicle. Any moron could tell you that it's a lot cheaper and more reliable to use an existing ship. Good god - there's a crap load of Navy ships just wasting away in mothball.

Can anyone grasp the concept of having roughly three thousand engineers collecting a high salary while not producing anything? Make something; create some solution to neutralize an atomic bomb, build the next terrorist-fighting robot, but don't sit around discussing sports figures while waiting to be told what to do next. NAVSSES is a repair consulting organization, you ask some department to fix a problem on your ships, and they in turn respond by saying, they'll get back to you. In the meantime, the person you just contacted for assistance contacts someone else, and this goes on all the way up to the original shipyard that built the craft.

Listen folks, we are not in a major World War where so many engineers, like they have presently working at NAVSSES, have to be paid a forty hour week salary. And even if we were in a World War, those engineers should be stationed rubbing shoulders with the people in the shipyard's Design Division, the people laying out the next critical structural piece.

If I'm not mistaken, I believe a few years ago like 2004, NAVSSES was contacted regarding the designing of the next generation fighting ships. I wasn't privy to the specifics, only that we were about to be saved from closure with the multi million-dollar deal. After all was done, I believe the dealmakers saw that NAVSSES had no capability to design anything. At best NAVSSES only has a handful of CAD computer programs, like four each. The multi million–dollar deal quietly disappeared and the place heard no more. The truth be told, the place is in a slow inevitable death.

MIDDLE EAST

The war in the Middle East is about fighting a spreading virus of Muslims with an agenda. There is no World War. The true crux of who is keeping the war going in the Middle East is none other than the Saudis government. The Saudi perpetrated nine-eleven; Saudis have been killed, and or arrested in Afghanistan and in Iraq fighting against Americans. The Saudis have for ages funded Madras's, brainwashing schools to teach children to despise and kill Americans and all non-believers. The Saudis government to this day freely publishes literature in the United States to kill Americans, and this is after several years that they were told by the State Department to cease publishing such literature. The Saudis government still enslaves and tortures people they deem a threat, and it was the Saudi government that gave sanctuary to the Mass Murder Idi Amin. They even flew in planeloads of whores for him, from his former country in the Congo. If anyone knows where to find Ben Ladin, it is the Saudi government. And even if they don't know, which is unlikely, they speak the same language and can easily locate him if they truly cared about helping the American people.

While nut job Muslims throughout the Middle East torture, abuse and kill innocent women at will, the Saudi government, which is suppose to be the keeper of the religion, do and say nothing against such abuses. In other words the Saudi government should be setting an example.

Al-Qaeda is not the crux of the problem in the Middle East. It's the Muslim leaders that are directly responsible for the worldwide spread of suicide bombers and the heinous barbaric treatment of women and children. Suicides and the repression of women by lunatic mullahs have become a means to an end all, and it's happening at an increasing rate to which the world has never seen.

The way the Saudi and Iranian government is repressing it's citizens into believing in something they may not wish to believe in, is by using physical force, imprisonment, beatings, and murder. Not once, has the keepers of Mecca spoken up against atrocities commented against women, suicide bombers, decapitations, public stoning, women's genital mutilation, brainwashing children to hate and kill, and this list of demented Muslim norms is endless.

If it suits a sick man's mind, the Muslim leadership throughout much of the world seems to find a way to sanction the demented abusive behavior, as long as the behavior is against women and children. Women throughout much of the Middle East are treated no better than a goat under twisted sick interpretations of Islam and the Saudi says nothing to stop it.

It seems that every 6 months or so, a law is passed in the Middle East to repress women further into obscurity to become zombies, the walking dead, for man's sole pleasures as he sees fit, even to unbridled perversions.

Can't the World Court see that much of the Middle East, especially in Saudi Arabia, Afghanistan and Iran, that these governments are based on a questionable repressive religion? Their governments are nothing more than cults run by some mentally sick masochistic individuals. It's time for the World Court to begin arresting some Mullahs before millions more innocent people have to die from such evil leaderships. These psychopathic leaders believe themselves to be Gods, hence the willingness of the citizens to become suicide bombers. The only time the Saudi government takes action against Islamic terrorist is when it affects the repressive government of Saudi Arabia – period.

I pray that the next President ceases all future arms sales to the Saudi Government. Had it not been for the Madras's, the schools of hate, funded by Saudi Arabia, along with other hateful racist religious teachings, 9/11 would have never happened. The Saudi and Iranian government are cowardly hiding behind religion in order to brainwash a whole society to becoming puppets as suicide bombers. What is occurring throughout much of the Middle East is no different than what occurred at Jones Town under Jim Jones the cult leaders. Stop the madness now or the wars in the Middle East will go on forever. Al-Qaeda justifies their sick behavior to what the multi-headed hydra leadership in Saudi Arabia sanctifies - period.

When it's all done and settled in the Middle East to where there can be some dialog, mark my word; the Saudi government will be investigated, and they will be found to be responsible for funding the majority of the terrorists throughout the world. The Saudi, not the Iranians are funding and supplying training and material for roadside bombs and suicide belts. The proof of suicide bomber training and supply was recently published in the local newspapers in May 2008. In the article, it said that the person training young boys to become suicide bombers was a Saudi. It's time for our Government to make the Saudi Prince stand in bare feet on his own hot sand and make him tell the truth.

And from a slew of writings whether it is some Moslem Theologian, Arafat the Egyptian terrorist to an article in the New York Times. Time and time again, there have been published writings about nut job Arabs and how they lie about anything and everything in order to achieve the end result of killing non-believers, even if it means annihilating the innocent too.

Like they say, "While not all Muslim are terrorist, the majority of murders of innocent women and children are committed by Muslim. Muslims will murder their own children, especially if is a girl, because of a twisted monstrous cultural mindset that suggests women are property, not people. Never before in any of the modern wars have so many innocent children and women had their throats cut as there exist under Islamic cult teachings. And there is more...

I'm glad to say that I have had several of my letters to the editor from several local newspapers published. The majority of my letters condemned Islamic ways of murdering the innocent. Surprisingly, today July 19, 2008, I had another one of my letters published.

Here is that article as it was published. It was titled Cheers for a Killer; Israel frees a notorious murderer, Samir Kantar, killer of a 4-year-old girl and three others, in exchange for two murdered Israeli soldiers ("Uneven Mid-East swap draws cheers, anger, "July 17). The killer is welcomed home as a hero, with flags waving in celebration. What do you expect from people who sanctify the killing of innocents as part of their religion? The celebration of a murderer is part of their seventh-century mindset. This is one of many of my anti-Islamic letters I get published; I will do so until I see the Saudis speaking out and cease repressing anyone, not just women and children. So you see, I've been writing letters for years, I get involved; I don't let a cult like religion slide like the CIA did and still does.

And whenever a Muslim challenges me, all I have to say is that my Prophet didn't have to hold a sword to the peoples throat to make them believe in one God. My Prophet healed the sick, raised the dead and saved soles, and said that he spoke to God; on the other hand Mohammed fought in battles taking lives and riches, and said he spoke to God. Who do you believe?

Cult of brainwashing or religion, which is it. When you have to force people by fear of death to believe in anything, don't try to convince me that it is a religion. Where in our Constitution does it say it is ok to kill non-believers? Islam is a religion that sanctions slavery, the repression of women, the murder of daughters and everything that is ugly to freedom, how is it that they are allowed to continue to practice in the United States and the free world? Forcing women to stay covered is slavery, period. Brainwashing children to hate and to treating women as second-class citizens is against the constitution of the United States. If Islam as some followers have interrupt it, had been a religion of sacrificing animals like cats and dogs in this country, the American people would be up in arms. Witch Craft was a form of religion, and we know what happened to those women in our history. Where is the freedom as guaranteed by the Constitution of the United States for many Islamic brainwashed children and repressed women?

If all Islamic practices are a religion, why couldn't the KKK, the Skinheads or the Hell's Angels form a religion? That way the FBI and the CIA couldn't bother them, anymore than it interferes with Muslims murdering daughters or wives under false pretenses, or arrange their marriages as if auctioning off a goat. After all, everyone knows that you cannot go to Saudi Arabia wearing a crucifix, because frankly they are a racist people, not much different than the Nazi. You can get killed wearing a crucifix over there. They don't want the people to know the truth about other Prophets and religions. It's a brainwashed society. No, I'm sorry but when there is a religion that forbids questioning itself like Islam does with the Koran, or speaking about their questionable Prophet, then to me, it is no different than any of the cult religions like Jim Jones and the Jones Town Massacre and others like it.

Whole schools filled with girls have been locked and the girls inside burned alive. Women are being tortured and murdered everyday by Moslems for the most trivial reasons and the keepers of the religion, the Saudi's, say nothing or do nothing to stop it. And our President in 2008 wants to sell them five billion dollars worth of military arms. Isn't that sale making us complicit to the killing and torture of innocent women throughout the Middle East? Yes Americans, we are responsible for all the innocent deaths in the Middle East, because of some fat cats in the United States selling arms to people with a culture locked in the 6th century. The Saudi government has picked up the baton from the Nazi, and they are using American technology and weapons to go after Jews and all other non-believers to boot. If you don't like it, then start complaining to your representatives. It's the only way it's going to stop. I'm doing my part.

Throughout the world if there is a war going on, or there are people suffering, you can bet that terrorist Muslims are in the equation. Who let these terrorist people off the boat? Congress should answer my questions – show me in the constitution. Freedom means just that, it does not mean that anyone can repress, brainwash, enslave, threaten, kill or any of the norms that Islam preaches. No one can talk about or publish a cartoon in this country of Mohammed because of the possibility of Islamic threats. And we call this a free country. Free to whom?

Muslims should feel comfort in knowing that crap loads of Catholic priests have had to face the music, and that Mullahs are not far behind. OK, I could go on but that is for another book. Now that I got that off my chest...

BUNGLING ENGINEERING EXAMPLES

Here is a prime example of some the engineering bungling that I witnessed while working for the shipyard. This might sound trivial but this is just one of many such stupid engineering mistakes. It involved rebuilding one of the major piers that lead into one of the many dry-docks. Major water piping and sewage piping were laid in the pier form, prior to the concrete being poured. The plumbing was installed to service the ships docked pier side. Shortly after the concrete set all the embedded pipes moved, because of the differences in expansion between the two materials. Suddenly, all of the internal pier plumbing became useless. Too costly to replace - new pipes were laid to rest on top of the pier whenever a ship was docked. What the so-called expert engineers failed to realize was that they should have installed the pipes within a pipe, thereby eliminating the stresses on the service plumbing. A most basic engineering concept was ignored. And in the end, hundreds of thousands of man-hours, money and time were squandered over a most basic mistake.

Another bungling - NAVSSES was notorious for laterally moving machine shop supervisors and managers to an office environment, whenever there was a reduction in workforce in the shops. Rather than offer these laid-off guys a reduction in pay to remain working, they were able to keep their high paying salaries as office workers. On the surface it all seems innocent, until you stand back and look at the big picture. Here I was along with many others, with all this office experience writing messages, writing purchasing orders and contracts for labor, plus more, and the Navy drops this person into our section with zilch knowledge about any of the paperwork system. Not only were the shop guys getting paid more to know less, these unfair promotions or lateral moves undermined the ability or more deserving individuals from advancing. It just didn't seem fair. Most of those shop guys would have been more than appreciative, to have a job in an office atmosphere with the understanding that over time, that they could start receiving comparable pay and promoted further.

A different kind of discrimination:

Here is something interesting about the military. The Supreme Court ruled unanimously March 6, 2006 that the government can force colleges to open their campuses to military recruiters despite university objections to the Pentagon's "Don't ask, don't tell" policy on gays. So the Military can holler discrimination, but technicians cannot claim the same when denied promotions. After all, if secretaries or a technician can do the same work at many of the military departments such as at NAVSSES, as an engineer can do, why does the military continue to discriminate against the technicians? Let us not forget that the majority of engineering graduates, or I should say those that can afford to attend college of engineering, are statistically the well to do Caucasian whites. Is that not a form of discrimination?

Isn't this why the military suddenly decided to eliminate technicians from the playing field? The Navy understands that by hiring only engineers', minorities will stand little chance at landing a job with the Navy. It's true whether you like to understand this fact or not. Plus, it's understandable that by eliminating the technicians from working side by side with the engineers, there won't be any technicians to complain about equal pay for equal work, which is what the Navy is trying to do, and it's what this book is basically about amongst other human rights abuse issues.

So what's wrong with paying the person with the degree more than the technician doing the same work? Well for one, the taxpayer is getting a bum deal for taxes paid. To keep the engineer on a higher salary for the sake of using them at some future date doesn't exactly make sense either. By the time that engineer is called on to do some major calculations, he would have forgotten much of what he learned in college. In the end, the military will seek the expertise from an outside contractor to do what the overpaid engineer/ secretary was being paid to do. In this day and age with the Intranet all sorts of consultants and expertise exist on the web to assist on call. The military is delinquent for doing nothing to tap into this vast valuable engineering source.

It would take nothing to setup a website for anyone to go to, to solve some engineering problem that the Navy might want solved with a monetary award attached to it. Thereby eliminating a slew of card playing bored to death engineers, presently taking up space at NAVSSES and other such military organizations.

In other words, an engineer at NAVSSES is like an Olympic athlete let's say, and he has received his metal/degree for his for years of endearment. But like all past athletes if they are not continually exercising will become like any commoner on the street. But there is a difference when you work for the military, and that is that you will continue to receive top salary for what amounts to secretarial work.

What I find is wrong with the way the military is heading by only hiring engineers, is like placing blinders on a horse. There is no way an engineer right out of college understands anything about survival like a self-made street smarts person.

CIA 9/11

Similar to some of the managers at NAVSSES are these prime examples, the snot nose experts working for the FBI and the CIA. They were the laughing stock of the world, and some of the top officials working for the FBI and CIA should be serving time for dereliction of duty. Many innocent people died because two major national security departments relied on a bunch of incompetent college degree blockheads, in the CIA and in the FBI. Nine Eleven should never have happed. Does anyone truly believe that some overpaid CIA official stationed in Afghanistan, let's say is going to venture into the terrorists backyard for information as they profess? A CIA agent is more likely to pretend to be in troubled areas, but the truth is, he's probably in some plush hotel taking it easy. Which explains how some sheep herding Bedouins were able to out smart us.

Oh sure, some individuals from the CIA were instrumental in helping to beat the Taliban in Afghanistan. But the CIA was dead wrong in showing a bunch of criminal terrorist how to make roadside bombs and booby traps, which any moron would have known that someday that same training would be used on American troops. And it was irresponsible of the CIA to hand over as many stingers missiles without some form of self destruction built inside of them, that would have prevented communist China and others from reverse engineer the weapon. And what about the FBI failing to find a large cash of explosives at Tim McVeigh's house in Oklahoma? Plus the FBI had several incidents where their offices, especially the one like in Washington D.C., that were wide open to the public, to where anyone could walk in with a gun and shoot up the place, what morons. Professionals, I think not, naïve and idiots at best, and the Navy continues to make similar mistakes – read on.

So back to my Navy stuff, the bottom line problem with the way the Navy runs business is that it doesn't have to answer to anyone. It doesn't matter to them, because they don't have to show a profit or results. None of the Naval NAVSSES managers, which I worked under, could survive in the private sector, oops unless it was for a contractor with a Navy contract. Try putting any one of my past managers on the television show, The Apprentice, and it will be the comedy of the century. Those same managers can only survive at another job after retiring by working for one of the contractors, contractors that had dealings with the Navy. One hand washing the other in a slimy muck of slithering eels in a mating ritual – that's the way I viewed such questionable mating slim balls - double dippers. It's collusion and unfair competition to all other businesses not privy to so much inside information, not to mention favoritisms. For instance, when the director retired and went to work as a contractor bidding on projects that he knows too well, what are someone else's chances against such odds?

And then there is the manager from the procurement/purchasing department who retired in the middle of several complaint of discrimination, and returned to work the following week as a contractor in another NAVSSES department. The reason given for this person being immediately hired was that NAVSSES was short of knowledgeable purchasing agents. Is the Navy really getting a fair competitive buying with such collusions? Actually, to begin with, the only people of NAVSSES had to fear was the man in charge of the purchasing department. He made purchasing the most basic item, a nightmare from his paranoia of that mysterious beyond NAVSSES control agents, which might reject one of his reviewed over a thousand times purchases. So everything and I mean everything on a purchase order or contract for services, had to be edited and re-edited until the ship's engineering officer requesting the item or service would give up waiting, and purchase it them selves.

What the Navy needs is a panel of buyers that do just that. That way there would be no mistake and much of the ridiculous paperwork would reduce to a simple template requiring minor tweaking. Items such as non-stocked nuts and bolts for God sake, why have to write up a lengthy paperwork and then have to wait months to receive them. When a panel of buyers could easily pickup the phone or send out and email to buy them.

And it wasn't just the purchasing department that was creating obstacles to simple buys. Many of the Supervisors and managers were just a guilty from lack of supplying job orders on time, to ridiculous editing of the purchase orders and contracts. Some of them were even guilty of supplying expiring job orders knowing full well that the purchase would never materialize, and then use the loss of the buy against the subordinate when evaluating his PARS. No matter, because the PARS were somewhat illegally setup so that the employee could not contest whatever his supervisor wished to put down. Did anyone in the directorship review the PARS? Are you kidding, how could they with several thousand employees PARS to look over?

So what you have during the annual evaluations processes, is supervisors and managers nit picking subordinates for something as trivial as forgetting to look at some spreadsheet with useless information and such. But when the same manager fails to respond to a subordinate's request for funding or to sign a message – well, that's ok because the manager's PARS are off limits to the subordinate. A manager can come to work with a Robin Hood green T-shirt or in something that looks like Halloween pumpkin orange T-shirt, but if a subordinate shows up with a similar yard sale looking outfit, you can be sure that the manager will dig up something to downgrade that persons PARS.

When a mistake is made, as usual, only the people building the pyramid get crushed under one of the rocks. Or how about this, NAVSSES clubs the subordinated people like baby seals to cover up the management bungling system with annual $7000 bonus costs. That's what it felt like working for NAVSSES. Somehow, the department's managers have this mentality that the technicians job is to know and understand the physical equipment, but the technicians are not smart enough to know how to fix them or to come up with a solution to fix them. And that only those covered in dead seal pup skins can metrically understand how to fold their paper degree into an origami solution to the ship's problem.

PARs cannot evaluate a persons mental state or any of his health conditions, family matters and a whole slew of intangibles, too many to list them all here. If a person has some family hang-up going on at home or discovers infidelity, or is upset because someone else receives a promotion for equal work, how the crap is the stupid PARs evaluation of a person's work ability going to assess any of that? I don't know of a single person that who would say anything if they had one of the mentioned ills for fear that everyone in the place would find out. People like to gossip – we all know it. Managers and supervisors are no different. Besides all that – PARs can be tweaked by the supervisor any way he wants the outcome to be, just by manipulating the questions, assigned jobs, time factors and so on.

And what about a persons mental abilities, whatever happened to assisting the handicapped? Did NAVSSES suddenly decide via PARS to downgrade some individuals that unknowingly harbor a lower IQ than some other person? For instance; if you were to ask some of the people in private, about how they felt about a woman's ability or a Black persons ability to excel in certain areas, do you suppose, that you might discover facts that you might not hear from the same people, if that same question was asked in a public forum? Let me put it another way; how many of you have children with lower IQ's or have some semblance of retardation? If you do, do you tell that child he's retarded or slow, or do you build him up as if he were an equal to all others around him?

At NAVSSES we all came to work on an equal par, you might say. By that, it means that you do not talk down to someone that may exhibit one of the above-mentioned mental handicaps. And yet, here is an evaluation system adopted by the Navy to in some way, tell a person, that he is stupid. Now, the way I see it, if we were all doing what amounted to the same kind of work, why not award and pay everyone equally the same. Why should some with perfect whatever as the Navy sees it, be promoted and awarded, while at the same time stabbing the less than individuals in the chest with questionable PARS? The whole process is NAVSSES's way of exorcising a person's self esteem via condescending comments. "So you see here Johnson, the reason I gave you a lower rating this time on your PARS was because you forgot to look at Leslie's spreadsheet last week," What a mud head, and to think that the director claims to have reviewed the PARS results.

When it came to my level of understanding people and work assignments, if anyone was lacking in mental abilities it was always one of my managers and or my supervisor. I should include the director and captains for not doing a better job at coming up with a more equitable way of evaluating people. Say ex-captains shouldn't you be throwing away some of your phony chest bling? Yes - I lowered my standards in order to communicate with pretty much all of our captains whenever I had dealings with them.

Say what you may, but some of my best friends while working at NAVSSES were the less than or mentally slow/challenged. They at least get up everyday to earn a living without thinking about creative ways to get away from work.

So at one end of the spectrum NAVSSES recruits the inexperienced right out of college, and lavishes them with phony awards followed by promotions, and at the other end NAVSSES implements a PARS system to punish, demote and threaten to fire all others with the seal of approval – nice. You think maybe - no? Well - take a look at the people who received downgraded PARS and compare them against the pedigreed.

This is most evident by the huge disparity between awards handed out to the engineers' verses awards handed out to the technicians - if any:

An example of how the Navy operated in my opinion; can be best be described by what the famous British Commander Montgomery observed while commanding a bunch of young recruits during WWI. He noticed that no one up his chain of military command had a plan to win the war. In the past, Great leaders always had a plan for beating their opponents. Montgomery's men in the trenches were being slaughtered because of a bunch of officers too far removed from the front lines. It was exactly the way I was working day after day at the shipyard and at NAVSSES. In the end, the shipyard closed. Much of it was because no one in charge had a plan. Funny isn't it, how private shipyards can manage to get funding year after year to build ships, and yet the Navy in Philadelphia flounders like a squid in the desert as it tries to find funding. NAVSSES has reverted from a flounder to a jellyfish with a bunch of useless sandy tentacles.

Navy officers must feel like they have accomplished something after having received as many metal bling pinned on them, as there is weight in a bronze ship's propeller. Was the Captain of the USS Stark busy polishing his metals just before suicide bombers attacked? Were the terrorist permitted to get close enough to his ship because they were mistaken for divers jumping in the sea after tourist coins? And was the Commander in charge of Pearl Harbor busy pinning his shirt metals while the Japanese were lining up their aircrafts for dive-bombing? People - officers training my ass…

OUR DIRECTOR

When is the military-Navy going to promote a director that gets down in the trenches with his men, instead of promoting some guy because he's dressed for a catwalk? A diploma and a suit, especially a coffin gray suit like our director wore everyday, such garb never made a great leader that I'm aware of. Our director was afraid/xenophobic to make public speeches, and he said so publicly when he had to. Our director was more adapted or fit to be a mortician than a director of NAVSSES. Just before the director's retirement, my manager issued an email for more people to make an effort to attend the directors retirement dinner. "Look, this man did so much for us by keeping this base open during the BRAC hearings."

Oh sure, if the director spoke up at the BRAC hearing, he did it to ensure he had enough time in for his own retirement; plus where's my promotion? In the end, it seems, nobody really cared to see him off. Supposedly, one close friend of mine even mentioned to me that he called this same retiring director an ass hole via an email, because the director was being so arrogant regarding some issues about employee dissatisfactions in the place. I know it be true because the director said the same thing to me, "Quit if you don't like it."

Actually, when I retired after 39 years and I would have stayed until I had 40 years in the business had my manager behaved himself? Anyway, not a single person from the director to the captain came over to shake my hand on the day I left the place. Which only demonstrates, just how much the over paid buffoons really care for their people. At the retirement gala of others that I attended, the only idiots that spoke positive about working for the Navy at NAVSSES, either were the over promoted for their abilities, or those too stupid to have held a similar well paying job position on the outside.

Many of the upper management personnel were reluctant to make changes or to suggest new ideas for fear of failures. Once they achieved their promotional goal, none of them were about to upset the cart. This is not the way a successful business succeeds. A good director and or captain should understand that employees have issues, such as stress and the unthinkable whenever change occurs. And NAVSSES was guilty of this big time, with its constantly changing organizations and moving managers around. The people to look up at were no longer there, which added to the confusion and messing up the employees moral, not to mention the newly promoted blank skulls void of ideas or experiences, thus sending trust bumping against the logs circling the drain.

At NAVSSES a comic like Woody Allen would have made a more appropriate director. At least we could have all had a good laugh. I never recalled a single all hands meeting, where any of the leadership rallied us all together for a pep talk about things happening in the future. It was always an all hands meeting of what might be happening to us, as dictated by some outside force making all the decisions.

"Gee Fellas, it looks like the higher ups are requesting we cut back this or cut back that, and I'm not sure we're going to have a job tomorrow?" Every one of our stinking meetings were either depressing or another reorganization, that was suppose to appease some gods in Washington, or some invisible forces from another military-Navy division like Carderock. What a bunch of losers, my upper managers were, and I'm sure they still are. Like I indicated earlier- with all the engineers hired to work for the Navy, there is no reason why an aircraft carrier isn't flying instead of still plowing through waters, and taking days to get to it's destination while wasting gazillions of gallons of precious fuel.

It took a private contractor to design a future magnetic aircraft launch system - not the Navy. Hell, I designed such a toy when I was 8 years old. I was firing steel rods with the toy I designed and winding my own motors from whatever I could scavenge. I had a curiosity like that of the famous Robert Hooke's, inventor of the microscope and more; I wanted to know how everything works. Once I understood a particular subject, I did not dwell on it, instead I moved on for more challenges. Unlike many of the sports fans that tend to understand not only how the dimples of a ball for instance affects it, they can tell you how a sports player picks his nose, and they often will follow the player as if that person were a God. Sounds like many of the NAVSSES employees?

But the Navy cares to only listen to boys with some diploma notarized with an imprinted resembling some sphincter impression, and or the sports enthusiast who can recall last night's sports score. Ah yes, the diploma boys come to work after just breaking away from mommy's apron. They should be able to help out the Navy - after all; these boys come to work with a handful of cranial synapse connections, which are all the Navy requires. No one bothers to ask the new recruits about past creative works, hobbies, and such. Got a paper, you're hired. Got a paper and can talk sports you get promoted. A diploma is nice if someone else is hired to come up with creative designs, or new and efficient ways of managing the Navy. That way, the person with the diploma can be utilized for his skills to compliment the new creative designs. But it isn't so. If it were, why are we still plowing the waters using the same fuels and or the using the same drive train for propelling the Navy crafts through water, whereas private individuals unrelated to the Navy are coming up with some of the most outstanding creations ever designed.

I'm not proposing that we do away with such departments as NAVSSES. I'm saying that if the Navy needs engineering advice to do on going repairs for the existing ships, what's wrong with asking the shipyards that built them? NAVSSES is so remote from the shipyards regarding construction and how they function internally, it doesn't make sense to continue to use the NAVSSES facility. As a research facility it might work, but first someone in Washington has to provide funding to do specific researching. To assume the experts of yesterday still exist at NAVSSES, you have to be kidding yourself. For one they're all gone or just about ready to retire. What is left is a bunch of young recruits, and women promoted to equal the playing field with not the foggiest idea of the construction of ships, let alone how the engines work, or how the complex electrical system is networked throughout the ship. No – I'm sorry, but if you want your ship fixed, go directly to the shipyards that constructed them. For answers, bypass NAVSSES and save time and money.

Employees at NAVSSES became fodder for upper management to abuse with pseudo ghostly mannerisms. Anyone discovered to be complaining or questioning management could be made to travel a disproportional amount of time as compared to the others. They could be assigned the most difficult jobs while others were free to play poker or review sports stats on their computers, all day long. Training or special classes could be denied from those they deemed to be non-players. I was there 35 plus years and some snot nosed kids recently out of school were given cell phones and I-pods to use, and the freedom to pretty much travel where ever they wanted.

But not me – I couldn't be trusted. Some of the most recent hires were so useless they were often seen just walking from one building to another to kill time. I recall that one of them had a comical dance step when he walked. Each one of his steps was accentuated by lifting off with his toes making his gate appear to be bouncing in a sine wave. The other engineering guy had a long laid back gate as if he were trucking. Both were a laugh to watch during my lunch break. The promenading outside wasn't unusual for only one out of ten individuals had any serious work to do. I would at times stop by the electrical division for some information, only to see some of the engineers bored to death from having nothing more to read other than the same technical manual for months at a time.

It seemed like once the young engineer graduate from engineering college they were hired to monitor data that eventually ends up on a graph. Doctors do doctoring right out of college, and they get better with time. Navy engineers lose all ability to do engineering within 5 years; their engineering knowledge becomes atrophied. No one challenges them once they're hired to stay at their engineering peak. The box the Navy creates for its people needs to be empted like a cat's litter box.

CAPTAIN AND MORE

Our phony Captains, and we changed command quite a few times, advertised that they all had an open door policy. But whenever I would email one of my concerns to them, more often than not it was either ignored or brushed aside with a brief stupid response. If that weren't bad enough, if my complaint was about a supervisor, I would get a nasty gram from my super too for not talking to him first. There was no true open door policy. It was all phony, but it looked good for the Captains to be saying so.

For the amount of pay the Captains were receiving, it never made any sense to me that they should get paid so highly for generic memos I saw them put out. Ninety percent of the Captains memos would say something like, Drive safe during the holidays, don't forget to add water to that Christmas tree, and such 7th grade verbiage. Anyone of the Captain's memos could have been pulled from catalog of high school business letters. The majority of us deleted his emails the instant we saw them appear without even reading them. We didn't have to read them, because the Captain had a long line of managers and supervisors, including secretaries that would send us that same garbage the captain just issued, just so they could all appear to be working or have something to do. The majority of upper management offices were always void of stuff lying around indicative of someone with zilch to do. Steve Jobs, the head of Apple Computer, they were not.

At best, our Captains amounted to the seed pits, wannabe someone important. But alas, where was mommy to plant them into soil so they could flourish. A piece of paper and a ship's cruise at sea do not make a leader. Some of these guys had so much metal bling, that you would think that they were wearing a gaudy bulletproof vest, kind of like an 1800 South American ruler. The only things missing on their getup were a few gold teeth for that ghetto look.

A FEW OTHER ISSUES

A few things I would like to mention before closing. One is that if you haven't noticed my attitude for accomplishments have never been hampered – except for when I worked for the Navy. I always went after what I believed in and whenever something adverse happened - I quickly moved on to something else. Just like many of my projects, whenever I couldn't continue with one subject - I picked up another and kept on moving. I rarely had time to get depressed, because I could always find something new to learn or discover. The world and everything on it is too beautiful to let it go by, if I were ever blindsided. There is never enough time to get it all in from the deepest oceans, to mysteries of the mind.

How can anyone claim there is nothing to do? How can a person avoid retirement, especially from a do nothing NAVSSES, when the world crises out for help? Try; planting a tree, help the needy, write a song, clean the beaches, or just comfort the ill, but to do nothing is sinful. Stop being a user of this planet – contribute something. Even Jesus said, "Let the dead bury the dead." Why can't some people understand that concept? Stop wasting valuable time. People died yesterday and they will die tomorrow. Someday, we will all get time to see them in the here after. Now is not the time to dwell on trying to contact the dead.

Many of the old retired farts from the place where I worked returned as contractors. They're what I called losers.

These guys have zero creative abilities and seek something to do by latching on to similar work after leaving. "Oh, please tell me what to do because I need some direction." That's what they sound like. Not a single one needed the job to stay afloat, especially after receiving such a huge retirement from the Navy. If they still had a mortgage, a car to pay off, or some kid in school, shame on them for pathetic retirement planning. Sorry, but these guys just remind me of gluttonous packrats, squirreling away more money than they can possible use before the Grim Reaper comes knocking. And yet, the Navy invites these gluttons to privy contracts and technical specifications, normally hidden from competitive bidders. Is that fair?

THE E-MAIL

This is the actual email sent around our office and passed around to just about every department. Nothing at all was altered in the e-mail. This is one example of what the Navy deems was a competent Manager worth of $150,000.00 salary and multiple awards amounting to $7000.00 each. He sent this warning to his people under his control at the time. Oh my sides hurt just from reading it again - LMAO. What a dick! Oh, I'm sorry; his name was Billy Goat, not, short for his real name. This email has circled the globe via the Intranet, so nothing is secret about it.

Big brother is watching you. Name of sender omitted to protect the clown the Navy deemed fit to be a manager, but we know who it is. As I noted in my e-mail on BUSINESS ISSUES, it seems that the effects of my WARNING SHOTS e-mail has worn off. Furthermore there are are areas of concern that fall into the same categories of waste/inefficiency, poor work practices, ignoring or forgetting certain rules or flat out fraud. As a matter of discussion yesterday I went around the office at 1145 and found 3 people eating or making their lunches, and 5 were not at their desks. When I went around at 1235, 1 person was still "at lunch" and 3 were not at their desks. Last night I reviewed the timecards and sign in/out sheets from over the holidays and noted that of the 61 inputs, 44 (72%) of the people left exactly to the minute (or within 5 minutes) of the time required for exactly 8 or 9 hours depending on their schedules. Two people were short hours (1 due skipping lunch). Corrected timecards will be submitted. Two places sign in or outs were missing. Reviewing yesterday's time I found an erroneous entry (which was corrected) and a skipped lunch period (which will be charged to AL).

I've broken down the concerns as follows:

POOR/INEFFICIENT WORK HABITS
Walking around, BS-ing, generally not working

LUNCH TIME PRACTICES

going to "blind man's" early but still taking from 1200 to 1230 to eat lunch.

going out to "fast food" places and eating at desk well after 1230

taking longer than ½ hour for lunch still in Conference Room (eating, watching videos, whatever) after 1230

TIME KEEPING PRACTICES

working thru lunch when leaving early

not signing in or out honestly

some people are still not getting in by 0930 and charging leave

daily sign in/out sheets not being reviewed when time is verified

leaving early without prior approval

This is my plan for addressing all of the above ISSUES: (Everything goes into effect on Monday 1/13.)

My actions:

more walking around by me. Though I am more inclined to just sit in my office, it seems people are taking advantage of my lack of presence.

more monitoring and challenging of those not working/at their desk.

noting people not at their desks before lunch: eating lunches early but still using lunch time to go out or sleep at their desk, etc; eating lunch well past 1230; or in the conference room past 1230.

reviewing daily sign in/out sheets for errors, etc. including to see if people that took long lunches "flexed" to cover the longer lunch.

either 9760 or R D, only, will verify T.I.M.E adding sheet above sign in/out clipboard that lists, in 5 minute increments, correct end times for start times from 0530 to 0930.

once I come in, in the morning, I will take the sign in/out sheet into my office. People coming in and not finding it at the normal location on the little credenza, will find it on the table in my office.

at the end of the day when I leave, I will put the sheet back on the little credenza.

I will talk to people that I see routinely

BS-ing or not working,

not following the rules around lunch time or not compensating for longer than ½ hour lunches by "flexing" or taking leave.

After verbal warning, I will put it in writing and take disciplinary action, if not corrected.

Your actions:

For the record, lunch time is between 1200 and 1230. You MUST take lunch....it is not optional. This is not something I dreamed up but a legal requirement. I can not ALLOW you to not to take the ½ hour for lunch. (Besides most people DO eat their lunch, even if they're working through it.)

If you leave early but work past 1230, you can not calculate the ½ hour from 1200 to 1230 into your time charged to work.

charging at ½ hour increments for any time after an 0930 start.

leave should be planned/approved in advance. I understand that emergencies arise but in some cases I'm not hearing about it until I see the sign in/out sheet the next day. If I'm (or acting 9760 is) not around find Ed. If neither are around, give a note to one of us.

everyone in 9760 will sign in/out on the same sign in/out sheet.

This is the part I hate most about being a Supervisor. I consider it baby-sitting and I really abhor it. I'm not happy having to do these things and I'm sure it will show, but it's part of the job. I know things happen like people can't always eat from 1200 to 1230, or that all the good stuff is gone by 1200 if you wait to go to "blind man's". But to routinely go early and then still take ½ hour from 1200 to 1230 without "flexing" can't be tolerated.

It bothes me that this will likely inconvenience a lot of people who are the ones that routinely invest their own time and energy into their jobs, don't take advantage of freedoms and who deserve flexibility because they've shown responsibility in managing it, all because of those that don't care about the product, the cost or the group as a whole.

Everything above goes into effect on Monday 1/13. It will stay in effect until I'm convinced the problems are rectified or a new solution has been found.

Bill PS Today 7 people were not at their desks at 1150 when I walked around and one was making lunch. At 1235, 6 people were not at their desks and 2 were still "at lunch". 8 of the people were the list both days. I will be looking at the sign in/out sheets Monday to see who "flexed" to make up for it.

PSS If you have a better plan for dealing with these issues, I'd like to hear it.

That manager was so anal retentive, that his hairy dingle berried sphincter must have been in his throat. How he was picked for the promotion to supervisor and then manager, I'll never understand. Oh, I almost forgot, the Navy just looks to see if you have that toilet paper often referred to as a diploma.

During inclement hot weather, Billy Goat would often show up to work in his Robin Hood green T-shirt. He must have bought it a yard sale mixed in with the pet doggy clothing. A fine example of a $149,000 manager, he set for rest of us in the office. Oh yeah, here was a typical manager managing a mere five people for that kind of salary. Waste? I think so, especially when our section had two other people rated with a GS-13 salary and three contractors all performing similar work. Wake up Carderock, it's time to scale back some of the Navy satellites.

At one of our few meetings, I had a good face off look at the creepy guy, and that's when it hit me. He personifies Beelzebub, if there was such a head demon. His facial appearance with a goatee and matching mustache, along with the way his hair formed about his skull, were all the signs of a devil, disguised in human form. Shit – all he had to do was color his face red and stick on a couple of paper water cones on his skull, and he would qualify hands down in the stage play Faust. I might also add that his office space was decorated with gargoyles for real, which completed his personality.

Let's see, as I'm writing this book I have approximately 39 years working for the Navy. In all those past years, I do not ever recall a supervisor or manager penalizing the employees for attending a funeral for a fellow employee. Billy Goat did just that. He waited until everyone in my office left to attend the funeral, and then he put himself in the log sheets for 3 hours off in order to attend the funeral. Upon returning to work the following week, since the funeral was on a Friday, Billy had the secretary dock everyone that was at the funeral x amount of time off. This guy was the Time Monitoring Troll of NAVSSES.

By the way, I understand that someone recently wrote a book titled: The Lucifer Effect. In it, the author demonstrates how people when they come into power become somewhat evil towards subordinates. You see, when they are at home they are not always the boss.

Some of the guys from the office claimed that they saw Billy peeking over their booth, making them feel like someone was looking down on them in a public toilet booth. One of the employees complained that Bill suddenly appeared staring at him, just as he was plucking out one of his nose hairs. "What's up Bill?" You never knew, when he might look in for no reason at all. He had a sneaky habit of walking past a cubical, and then suddenly backtracking to catch the person in some silly whatever. Who can tolerate that kind of behavior from a managerial boss, day after day? He eyed the sign in, sign out sheets so close, that you could swear that his eyeballs blotted the paper. That was Billy Goat. Is this what the Navy wants as a manager? Some guy, who belittles and talks-down some of the best outstanding workers like myself with insulting demanding requests?

REALITY

As I look back to when I first entered NAVSSES, it just seems like more work got done when we were block funded. Not that pilfering, non-workers and such didn't exist. I'm not claiming they didn't work, but it wasn't a bunch of redundant pie charts and bar graphs like they now have. Only now, more is spent for micro managing every nuance of the all mighty devalued buck, while the bosses are discovering creative ways of stealing via perks and awards. The place has become an orgy of pay raises. No longer does a person recently out of college have to endure a few years of learning the ropes sort of speak, or have to understand such things as the difference between port from starboard or the meaning of 01 level and so on...

Now, don't get me wrong about some of the engineers that I worked with at NAVSSES. Work was getting done. It just wasn't what I considered engineering work. It was more busy work, numerous repeats of existing data and such.

The stupidity while working for the Navy at times was overwhelming. We all had to learn to live with it, because it was the best job out there at the time. Approximately, ninety plus percent of the engineers where I worked did zero engineering. Much of the work, or I should say all of the work was documentation, scheduling, pie charts and such. You could say the caliber was more secretarial work even technical in nature and nowhere was it engineering. A lot of the work did not require the services of an over paid engineer. As a matter of fact, secretaries were also frequently promoted to engineering pay scales, as I previously mentioned. These girls did the same paper shuffling, which more than proves my point.

About the only creative engineering I felt was going on while working for NAVSSES was having my office space moved from cubical to cubical or from building to building. It seemed like the managers couldn't come up with the latest and greatest new whatever, but they could always find funding to move us around like hyenas moving from a den that was too flea infested.

Consolidation was a word often used by the management to make it appear that the organization was saving money. We were consolidated from one code to another. Initially, when I came onboard with NAVSSES, my code was 0023. My code number had bounced several times every other year or so. I never knew what my new code was going to be. When I finally approached retirement status, my department code number settled somewhere around Code 918. I had enough sense never to buy my own NAVSSES business cards, when my manager at the time had asked us all to invest in them. And just as I suspected, the business cards became useless within 6 months, time and time again. Actually, there was one individual in my group who purchased his business cards sans any code number with a space to pencil them in. Pretty unprofessional looking wouldn't you say?

Can you imagine going from a code 0023 all the way to a code 918? How did that happen? It was as if some guy in Washington or our director was pulling numbers out of his butt. These are the managers that are supposed to be making intelligent decisions? Leadership is not toying with numbers and shuffling people around every 6 months. It's about getting the job done, advertising the business, coming up with new ideas, and carrying them out and most important - soliciting funding.

Many of the managers wanted the promotions for the monetary rewards, but they failed miserably when it came to going after the funding, or how to best utilize talented employees and contractors.

After the Navy shipyard closed, companies like Barco and Urban Outfitters and many others that moved into the shipyard all demonstrated superior creativity, engineering, and usage of facilities and buildings. While the property was under the care of the Navy, repairs on a building seemed to take forever to get done, and much of the Navy Yard remained pretty much the way it was designed, way back during the Second World War. The lack of improvements and repairs by the government was because the Navy required mountains of paperwork to get anything accomplished. Like I said, too many brain dead leaderships chasing after way too many pie charts.

AFFAIRS

Here is some additional proof of NAVSSES lacking leadership, and it involved employees having amorous affairs. One individuals was married with a couple of children had an affair with one of the red haired secretary (maybe dyed), and from that affair she had his child. You would think that someone from upper management would have said something to him. Nope, this same Romeo turned around, and had a second child with the secretary; all the while the Navy was paying for her time off... I need not go into the office turmoil the two created, whenever the fatherless secretary would get into his cubical and start a fight over everything, from child responsibility, to why he was still married to his wife. In other words, this guy had a pseudo harem going on. And it all seemed to be sanctioned by NAVSSES, because some of the supervisors were having affairs of their own too.

One in particular was between a married supervisor and his co-op trainee. The co-op got pregnant, so I heard, and ever after she would roll a couple of steel ball bearings in one of her hands while telling us that she had him by the balls. Needless to say, this girl, also was put in for the Chi Cola Award that amounted to a monetary bonus of something like $10,000, and she got much more. And if that wasn't enough, there were rumors that one of the directors had affairs with one of the boiler technicians at one of the local hotels, during working hours. This was all prior to being promoted up the way up to the zenith position. And here is story of one woman's ugly ordeal at NAVSSES, as she tells it

I started in SSES as a GS-4, Secretary in 1988. A year later I got promoted into a computer assistant job. A year after that I transferred to the now-Environmental Quality group. The manager there promised to pick me up on a detail, assign me equipment specialist work and then write me in as an entry level GS-5 equipment specialist, with promotion potential to GS-11. In 1993 I was promoted to GS-11.

There was a catch, though, no matter how much potential I had. I was expected to date my benefactor and Go to bed with him. I made no mistake about this. He used to call my house. Eventually, things soured because I never acquiesced. He pushed me off to other supervisors in the department. This GM-13 manager eventually turned 55 and retired. I made every effort during those years to learn the job. I traveled wherever they sent me.

His supervisor was never fond of me. He grew to hate me even more because the way I see it, I was the only woman technician in the group. While just about every male technician that management didn't absolutely hate got promoted to GS-12 via accretion of duties promotions, I was stuck at GS-11. And, my supervisor told me that he "Wouldn't necessarily promote me even if I graduated from engineering school." None of the male technicians had engineering degrees. I also supported the union while he was promising my coworkers promotions in lieu of helping him bust up the union. You see managers like him favored the new experimental program to get rid of the GS- system in favor of pay banding. That way he would no longer have to let people under him who he hated, get their step increases. Under the pay banding system, he could even cut someone's pay, just if they looked at him the wrong way. So, he would look the other way when one of his lackeys was out getting signatures on company time to decertify the union. The dissent effort failed and to this day the SSES engineers and technicians don't have pay banding. However, the people that helped him to get rid of the union miraculously got unannounced accretion of duties promotions to levels way past their career ladders.

After the shipyard closed, SSES only promoted via the accretion of duties Promotion Avenue – which conveniently bypasses fair merit principles by keeping the people they wanted to keep down from being able to compete fairly for a promotion. The management's original excuse was that they had to get around the stopper list from the shipyard. Today, even though the shipyard closed 12 years ago, accretion of duties promotions (a/k/a bag jobs) is still the method of choice since personnel and management don't have to acknowledge or defend their favoritism. But, that's another story.

Anyway, around 1997 I decided to go back to school and become an engineer. It was not easy, since I didn't have any math or science background. I just had a strong will to succeed. I eventually graduated in 2004 after so many grueling years of night school. All those eight years, I hung on a cliff while my managers kicked away at my fingers, trying to get me to quit school, because frankly, he didn't want to pay for it. In a meeting back in 1999, when the union representatives met with my GM 14, Ralph Rotten to discuss my going to school to be an engineer. It was then that he told them that the "bitch" (meaning me) wouldn't pass the courses and so therefore, he wouldn't have to pay for my school.

I kept plugging away at school after that. In my senior year, around 2002, it became very important that I travel 50 percent of the time. It was odd because they never required me to travel before. The idea was to motivate me to quit school since there would be no way that I could keep up with my classes at 50 percent travel. They tried to build a case around me refusing to travel. It was at that time that I was unofficially detailed to the program analyst position that was vacated by two GS-12 men before me. Since they refused to document it, they could also get out of giving me the pay and status associated with the GS-12 job. In June 2004 I finally graduated with a mechanical engineering degree. Ralph Rotten was humiliated and responded the only way he knew how. He conspired with the personnel hacks to force me to accept a demotion to a GS-7 engineer. It worked like this: no matter what I put on my application - the most I qualified for was a GS-7. I even filled out an application that specifically conformed to the OPM standards for GS-11 engineer!!! This was pure discrimination, since SSES had a history of converting technicians that finished school to engineers without forcing them to go down two grades. After all, I had the same qualifying experiences out in the fleet. I have a long list of guys in the good old boys club, who never graduated, but were converted to GS-12 engineers, and they were further promoted into GS-14 management positions. The personnel hacks at SSES are just that.

Most of them typically have a high school education but make in the neighborhood of 80K, which at the early millennium was 10K more than your averaged topped out GS-12 engineer or technician made. Was SSES a technical organization or what? The brains of the personnel department had a history degree and she was in charge of evaluating technical workers. They legally were not qualified to rate anybody since they were not delegated position examiners. They should not have been permitted to work onsite at SSES since SSES was never big enough to command their own personnel department. They were there for one reason only – to better perform the dirty work that SSES management wanted them to do – stuff that couldn't be done if the management had to work with OPM downtown. Whether or not someone was "qualified" to take a job really depended on whether the management wanted you to have the job.

Anyway, I actually saw the "brains" of the personnel department in a meeting with my two supervisors discussing what to offer me as a new engineer – which was a GS-7 with save pay and no guarantees of being re-promoted when the save pay period ran out. The amazing thing is how they made it look like they were offering me a great opportunity. It wasn't really an offer, when you consider that I had been a GS-11 for over 10 years. Yup, a GS-11, step 7. So – did Ralph Rotten wanted me to go from a GS-11, step 7 to a GS-7, step 11, or did he just want me to work at the Seven-Eleven??

I had filed an EEO complaint, which was in the pre-complaint phase the last month I worked there.   Basically, I was forced to work with some hack that was paid by the captain to discourage people from filing legitimate complaints, so that nobody would look bad. All he did was pass on insults and threats to me by the managers that usually hid under the desks when I walked by. The EEO lackey even told me that they were going push through paperwork making me take the GS-7 even if it was illegal. The idea was to wear me down.

To their surprise I quit and thanked the taxpayers, for the $38,000 they spent on my education. I must say I am doing better, however I was forced to walk away from a 16-year government career. This is the story that you will never hear from their PR department.

I forgot to mention that Ralph Rotten wanted to get rid of the union because the presence of a union that opposed pay banding was the only thing that kept out pay banding in SSES back in 1997 and until today.

And this, Geyer's infamous "bad people" remark (i.e., after pay banding went in effect for all the non-union people, Geyer was paraphrased as saying that he wanted to give bigger raises to some of his employees via the annual performance rating system, but the money came out of a finite pool and they were all his good people. He could not palm off any bad ratings to his so-called "bad people" because they were all in the union and not under the pay banding system. So, therefore, there was no money to appropriate to give to his "good people."

So there you go, and I could have added other such sad stories. It's not fair that a good portion of the technicians like myself took the time and made the effort to get a higher education only to be ignored as if NAVSSES management said, "So what." And this was from the director with a secretary making $90,000.00.

Security making little:
In light with the directors secretary salary is this: when I filed my papers to retire, I was appalled to hear from the women, who worked for security, that they were only rated a GS-6, making like $36,000. And do you recall what the assistant to the director was making? Sickening isn't it. Somehow I can see a person in security doing more work than someone that has to answer the phone and such. And if you don't think so, then take a look at the salary scale differences. It doesn't look like equal pay for equal work to me. Even the Blacks and Women on the outside demand equal pay for equal work. Why single out the technicians to get paid less or not be allowed to compete for the same promotions? NAVSSES should be setting the work standards and not leaving it up to the private industry.

SUPERVISOR CHANGES AND MORALE

Supervisors and managers came and went, and each change caused morale to tumble from the uncertainty of things to come. NAVSSES management meanwhile would sit back, and assume that the reshuffling will eventually morph into some highly motivated working unit. It was obvious that the place had no concept of how people react to change. People are like children, and as such they dislike a divorce, and that is what the organization was constantly implementing, on the very foundation of hard working people.

Some of it was done because a manager had an agenda to get himself promoted, by demonstrating that he was managing x-number of lower rated GS-13s. Many of the newly promoted tended to maintain status quote, and often they failed to realize that when you move up, responsibility increases. He now needs to shift gears and try something new. The newly elected supervisors fails miserably in getting to know the very people that they are suppose to manage. Much of it had to do with their own fears, like they don't care to know and others. I can't mention enough of how little my bosses understood what my abilities were. And it was dreadful to see an incompetent new employee be given a project that he wasn't familiar with.

To prove that technicians can be more than the Navy professes an example was the man who created the Machinery Alteration (MACHALT) program. He pretty much did it all by himself. No engineer here. He setup this program that is still some 18 or so years later, still revered by the people in the Navy. It's not often that a person like him comes along. Here was a self-made expert, a General Patton of Managers, with no engineering degree who showed-up the whole NAVSSES engineering department. He did what no other overpaid directors or managers could do. Yeah, whenever he had to impress upon anyone that might have made a mistake, he did it in such a way that could stripped away your hide. Maybe it wasn't the best way to do it, but you can bet that the person didn't make that same mistake in the future. This same creator of the MACHALT program would leave for Pearl Harbor, and be back the next day after a brief meeting with some Admiral out there. And there were many other pluses this guy did to prove that he was a better man, than any director I've ever known from NAVSSES.

WEBSITES

Speaking of websites, which I touched on, I should mention that my department at NAVSSES had one individual that was promoted to a high level, supposedly for his knowledge of knowing something about web design. So they put him in charge of it. The web site design was of 7th grade quality and so basic. When I redid much of it, and showed it to my immediate supervisor, with all the different ways it could be improved. It seems that the web design supervisor, wouldn't accept any of my suggestions on how to improve it least I embarrass him. It wasn't until the organization paid hundreds of thousands of dollars that NAVSSES website got a bit better, but it was still garbage for the money. Good usage of the employees – I think not?

They did the same for designing power point presentations. They hired an outside contractor to do their work. Like I mentioned earlier, many of them do not deserve such high engineering salaries, when much of what they do at NAVSSES is or was farmed out. I at least had a major medical company like Johnson and Johnson seek my advice from home business for designing some power point presentations. But not my work place at NAVSSES – oh no, my managers wanted to keep their attitude sticks up their butts at all times. No matter how much it hurt. They weren't about to concede, that I as a technician knew more about engineering then most of them clutching toilet paper diplomas - jerks.

I had numerous articles published in technical magazines and especially the local newspaper. At home my wife Jane keeps a stack of some of those articles. One of them that elicited ire from the FBI was printed in a Federal government magazine. My supervisor at NAVSSES at the time tapped me on my shoulder one day, and handed me a stack of publications about what I could and could not write about. And anything I wrote about that involved my job had to be cleared by my department. Well, I didn't think my article was so bad. I just got tired of reading articles in the newspapers about a lost FBI laptop with all sorts of secrets. I wrote to inform the public, that the lost laptops were crap at best with limited memory and abilities. As a matter of fact, I said we had a bunch of them ourselves just sitting in an empty booth. The best they could be used for was to play games. Years later after the 9/11 attack what I said in my article proved right. The FBI didn't have anything secret in those laptops, and anyhow, who in their right mind would put anything secret on them without some form of encryption, especially if you're working for the FBI, morons?

SOME ADDITIONAL FACTS

Statistics by David Halberstam in his book, The Best and Brightest explains that those who never go to school at all, the unschoolers, are on top of the heap socially, psychologically, intellectually, physically and even academically. Also Harvard studies show B students achieve more much later in life, than 'A' students, while C students often do the best of all. HELLO NAVSSES?

As proof that many of the people at NAVSSES were non-workers and or lazy – all the people I spoke to about this book, complained about the way the place was run and managed, but just a handful took the time to write something to contribute to this book. Just remember that. It was similar to the people that didn't sign up for the attrition settlement when the Union won big time against NAVSSES. Thank You John Garrity President of the Union, local 3.

More of Billy's Emails:
My Email to Billy Goat, a manager, in reference to a letter it seems only two of us in the department received. The letter was signed and the manager in a condescending verbiage sort of demanded this and demanded that from two of us. The letter made it sound as if the two of us were delinquent with some of our projects. I had always been prompt with my projects, and my work was always rated highly sat, and or just sat by all my previous supervisors when there was just two ratings (sat, un-sat). What could possible be bothering this new manager's problem? I knew it. He was the new chief, and pissed that he didn't get some other promotion. So he was going to kick someone for his loss, and he made the mistake of picking on me.

The Email I sent Billy - some names altered...
Both Johnson and I received this personal memorandum request it seems. Has anyone else been issued such a letter?

Also you and Franklin are well aware, per our meetings and emails that the tech codes responsible for said alts have been reluctant to respond (travel, priority, etc.). Franklin or Lesley has not provided funding of Job Orders for anyone or any code to respond to our request for information regarding the Brand New Alts (Job Order No?). You yourself said you were going to contact their managers/supervisors for some answers to my various alts. I still haven't received any information. Also, both Johnson and I haven't even received ILS data from QED on some of the alts as of yet, to even get a handle on what material to order. Franklin has not enlightened us as to which contractor is funded to assist with the prototype, and I can go on. If I call the field reps they tell me it's up to Franklin to pick a contractor, and they don't know who is going to get funded. The spreadsheet we received from Lesley (basically a cut and paste spreadsheet) had numerous mistakes and changes, and it wasn't even formatted to calculate totals for anything. Both Johnson and I returned a more professional updated spreadsheet with proper formulas installed. I keep getting the same questions asked over and over again from Franklin, Lesley, Mellow, Neely, and from you and others to fill in a repeat spread sheet with the same request (same stuff with color coding shuffled). Is anyone cross-referencing the information? You issued a prototype spreadsheet and expect an immediate response. My email to you regarding the status of the prototype spreadsheet was no more than a mere second after this one you sent...

You stressed a J&A be urgently developed for a 3 year contract with the OEM ATIS for MA515, which I did and placed in your in box. I heard no more about it. So which is it: I develop a J&A, I respond to a CASREP regarding the LHD-3 in Norfolk, I respond to Lesley's ever changing spreadsheet and others, or should I be in conference with someone in the electrical section for some answers to my alts? It's all work. I didn't realize your spreadsheet had priority.

I sent you detailed pictures from Paul Wary regarding the PLC upgrade for MA-634 and when I asked you if you even looked at them. You indicated you hadn't. Retrieving the information regarding the complexity of the HPAC PLC replacement wasn't a 2-minute meeting. It took a lot of teeth pulling from the ISEA to get a feel for what this alt entails. In the end, it seems this alt may just go away because of the material cost. The truth be told: had the person/manager responsible for developing the MACHALT understood the cost, maybe a lot of time could have been saved before it got to this stage. But hey, that's not my call. And last, let's not forget that my assigned list of MACHALTS; far exceed what you may have knowledge of. Every single past alt I was cog over; I still have to respond to, just ask Franklin. I just answered some for MACHALT 209 Terry Turbine Governor Valve Mods. You see, I wrote the 5 Technical Manuals regarding these alts as well the one for solid state circuit that fuels aircraft on carriers and many more. So when the ships force needs assistance they contact me. Even the ISE can't answer the field regarding some of my past alts; they too call me to respond. I suppose I could have said "talk to my manager - we require a Job Order before I can answer." But that's not what NAVSSES is about. And you know what? Not once has a single manager/supervisor recognized my outstanding work for developing the 5 technical manuals or the solid state fueling systems the carriers use to this day, including many others... Not to mention rebuilding high pressure steam governors on USS The Kitty Hawk while it was a sea for the 21 + days.

Are we expected to get more of these letters of attack?

And yes they are attack letters because you attacked our character before we were even given a chance to respond to your spreadsheet. Thirty-eight years in the business - I don't need to be addressed like I'm somebody new to how MACHALTS work. What ever happened to teamwork?

Larry Lueder

Sent: Tuesday, April 03, 2007 8:44

Subject: RE: Status Tracking

Importance: High

Another Email from Billy to Johnson and Larry,

You each have a number of prototype alts that need to get moving, so they can be installed this year. Instead of trying to meet weekly or even bi-weekly with each of you and Franklin IOT track I've developed the attached for you to use to track and report status. Begin using the attached and start reporting status weekly, either Friday PM or Monday AM. Copy Betty as well so he can keep the Field appraised.

Larry,

I also added the key events for the contract for ATIS to your list of prototypes, since that's critical too.

Billy 4/11/07

Shortly after Another Email from Billy

Guys, It says, "Begin using the attached and start reporting status weekly, either Friday PM or Monday AM." I got zippo from you as of COB yesterday.

Bill

Sent: Friday, March 23, 2007 10:53

Subject: Status Tracking

Notice above that it states for a status on either late Friday PM or Monday AM. And yet Billy throws a tantrum and bitches before the status is due. Plus he had a nasty twit of keeping records on each one of us, whenever we missed responding to his phony time schedule, and then used it against us later. The crappy part about all of this is that at the time, we didn't have any funding to get anything seriously done. The War in the Middle East - remember? Pooling recourses to nit pick some mistake with reams of documentation is nothing short of evil. Billy should ask himself if the way he deals with his people were the way he would like to be treated. I know for a fact that he was taken aback when I pointed out his mistakes, like failing to read my emails or given me my job orders before leaving on one of his trips and so on. Some how, it seems that when the people get promoted to any one of the managerial positions, they lose the ability to understand that to err is human. We all learn by mistakes.

In another Email from Bill Goat:

The manager, in one of his emails referred to the people in building 77L as the cesspool, April 24, 2007.

WORKING AT NAVSSES

Work at NAVSSES could at times be like a bad marriage with kids. You would like to get a divorce but there are children to consider. Show me the vision, the promotion; it was dull like a security guard pretending to guard during training, it's boring. Once elevated, the newly promoted had to find creative ways of telling the others why they weren't selected for whatever promotions or an award, etc.

And how often did I hear someone say this to one of the managers, "You think just because you were promoted to this position, that you all of a sudden you were more enlightened than the rest of us."

Get promoted to a managerial position in the Navy is like bubbling to the top. We were bubbles; some of us they would blow on to freely float in the air, and the others were left behind to rub about the crapped over gentiles and hairy asshole.

Working for the Navy in a civilian capacity as I saw it:
Management at Navy institute is best described as a committee – as an individual it can do nothing but as a group they decide that nothing can be done. I'm not sure who said that but that's NAVSSES for you... Face-to-face contact between management and the employees only seemed to occur during quarterly annual evaluations. And then management knows little about the person's accomplishments for the past quarterly term, and he knew even less about the person's vast mechanical knowledge and abilities. A phony dog and pony show mystically materializes (an all hands conference assembly) whenever someone has recently been promoted to a managerial position. It's all done to demonstrate and to proclaim/crown to those of us forced to attend, that the speaker is the new selected leader. He's the new lion-king on the block sort of speak; somehow I always saw them as a meowing pussycat that belonged on the Broadway stage show—Cats.

The problems with many of the Navy management promotions were that the people often promoted to such positions seem to lack talent; inventiveness, creativity, expertise and this list can go on. So how do I know all this? I know so because of what I saw over 39 plus years and from what the majority of employees were saying about the place all around me—day in and day out. Once a person was promoted to manager they often morphed into a know-it-all monster becoming obnoxious, closed minded, conceited, hotheaded, a windbag, vindictive or anal retentive and so on. None of these terms says anything positive about the managers, but these were some of the words used to describe them by many of the employees cowering under the new lion-king's paw.

Complain to the Captain about an abusive supervisor or manager and you set yourself up for retaliations that come in subtle forms such as obstacles to promotions, your annual rating suddenly drops, you're constantly pressured for useless status reports, your every movement is monitored and questioned and this list can go on.

Leadership is not watching some time clock to ping an employee's arrival and departure minutes, but this is the type of management that Navy seems to have a lot of. Where is the creativity in leadership, the new ideas, the Wow! Where is the sunshine, the smell of fresh baked bread, or the salt that flavors the food? It is as if the place is a nursing home serving unsalted puree for the toothless—bland, convalescing in a gray institute of some lower life forms incapable of constructive design. Instead, the institute flounders in a slow death as it seeks a breath of fresh air, all the while the mane-less lion prances about with a set of hearing aids sans the batteries. The institute begs for a safari of hunters to cull off the toothless, which tends to be dangerous to the overall advancement of leadership and technology, and if that is not possible may, I suggest a toilet brush through managements set of hearing aided ears.

SURVEYS

Surveys–let me tell you about some of the surveys, that the Navy squandered huge sums of money on. Surveys were initiated to put out feelers about the mood of the employees for such information regarding work quality, and or to discover facts about the management.

The truth was, that the truth about the surveys were never reported to cover up the true hatred, that the employees were feeling about everything from promotions to the anal retentive mannerisms, of many or the higher ups. Surveys were given as a phony way of allowing the employee to vent. Even the way awards were issued was a concern to many. For instance, the meat of any production manifests itself from the employees moving the stones to build the pyramid, but in the end, it was the managers and supervisors that squirreled away the six digit checks in secrecy, and it was done so as to not offend the technically savvy underling. So while the lower graded employees were awarded sufficient monies to purchase a roll of toilet paper, managers on the same project with zero hands on, often-received three to seven thousand dollar awards. Fair–I think not.

There was a survey that I took about one of their new website designs. They asked my opinion and I responded that a seventh grader could have done better. Well, you can imagine, I guess I hurt their feeling for them to respond. "You didn't have to respond in such a negative fashion." Oh really, and why not, after all I consider myself an expert in such field – I run a web design business. Spending thousands for what in-house employees could do – waste, I think so.

TOOTING YOUR OWN HORN

They say if you toot your own horn, that you are more likely to be promoted. The Noisemakers, not the nose in the grinding wheel gets the pay raise. For an institution that is supposed to pay the same for equal work, well it doesn't work that way for the Navy at NAVSSES. For instance, many of the technicians who were promoted to GS-13 positions, were most often promoted after handling a single large funded project. After that project was completed, it was status quo. In other words, the promoted person was now getting paid much more but wasn't handling an expensive project anymore. So why continue paying that person such a high salary? It doesn't work that way in the private industry.

And it wasn't fair to all the others working equally hard, yet they had a slew of smaller funded projects. Smaller projects that easily added up to multi-million dollar projects. Everyone worked just as hard and it had nothing to do with talent, because everyone was pretty much capable to some degree. The only ones that weren't, were the way too young and inexperienced technicians or engineers. But like I said, to assume that one person was better at carrying out a task over another in the same department was a joke, and the managers knew it. Somehow management felt that they were doing a just cause by promoting that one over all others, because large projects carry more attention getting.

I don't know how to relay the similarity between all the members working at NAVSSES; I suppose a close proximity is to compare it to people driving cars. When you look at the vast movement of traffic every night you go home, is there really a significant difference between one driver and another. Not really, in the end, one way or another, they all get home. It's this similarity that most of the employees feel cheated out of when they see others around them performing the same work, and yet NAVSSES randomly picks who gets an award and who gets promoted, projects be dammed.

Rocket Expert:

Von Braun Brown, the German Rocket scientist was an expert in his field. And yet this man was at the mercy of a bunch of jackass American military personnel, which were jealous of his abilities. Von Brown wanted to send up a satellite before the Russians did and more, but he was held back by inflated American officers. NAVSSES is playing this same game with the more talented and creative technicians, by assuming that a piece of paper equals more creative talent. And yet, there isn't an engineer at NAVSSES that uses anything that he learned about engineering, such as calculus, thermodynamics and chemical formulas. At best, engineers at NAVSSES use basic high school algebra, physics and rarely use chemistry and such.

ABOUT RETIRING

Managers were receiving 7K awards yearly while someone with 40 plus years receives zip at retirement. A plaque with your name printed on it with the number of years served, is barely worthy for such a devoted hard worker. Compare that against the ridiculous high salary and perks the managers receive, plus those phony outrageous awards, and you can see where much of the in-house hostility comes from. A nice retirement check would have made a lot more sense, don't you think?

It's very plausible that some of the suicides were the cause of the shipyard closing. Per the Army's record it had roughly 120 suicides in 2007. So while an employee at a lower level might have been fired for a simple infraction – the managers tend to get away with much worst theft from phony travel expenses to outrageous and phony overtime entries and more.

Demotions:
So while managers seemed immune from demotion – low graded rates such as a GS 10-11 or 12 could lose his job or be demoted. For example: I witness one individual that was hired basically right out of high school, and within less than ten years he was promoted to a GS 12 position. His two engineering bothers must have been instrumental in helping this much younger brother get hired and quickly promoted. So anyway, here was this inexperienced individual that was suddenly given a multi-million dollar job for the Army. I might add that my plea to my manager, that I should be handling such an extensive project went unheeded.

Shortly after, the young man on the block received his assignment; it all collapsed a couple of years later. And like much of the business at NAVSSES, it was all kept hushed up so I wasn't privy to particulars. But I do know that the department wanted to fire the young guy, and or demote him. In the end, the person opted to work for another department. His lateral to another section caused upset amongst those that were vying for a GS-12 promotion, which the new boy had just filled without competition. Was it right? I think not, and it showed mismanagement on the part of the manager and director.

Subordinates like the overly promoted kid right out of high school, underwent what irresponsible managers often do at NAVSSES, from their inexperience in how to properly manage. The multi million-dollar project that they placed on the kid's lap was like pushing someone out of a plane, with a parachute without any previous experience in parachuting. Yes, the kid had the tools, but without a foundation of experiences there's no telling where he's going to land, if he lands at all. The boy landed in a lake, and right off the bat the department manager wanted to fire the drowning boy, drowning him for sure.

The real person that should have taken the hit, when the inexperienced foundered with the major Army project was the manager, the same person who elected to assign such a huge task to someone with little or no experience. Too bad I wasn't asked what I knew about the circumstances. The boy received a threat of dismissal that he fought via assistance from the Union, and the manager received an award. But such are the dummying down of NAVSSES.

"Maybe next time, you'll be better prepared, it was my mistake. I should have done my homework before deciding to pick you to handle such an intensive project." That would have been the more responsible response from the manager, but instead like a cat in sandbox, the manager tried to cover it up by pointing fingers at the young man. NAVSSES was good at giving subordinates the finger. Weenie...

NAVSEA THE BAKERY

What NAVSEA requires is a computer program that highlights areas that require attention? Instead, what NAVSSES has are a bunch of spread sheets that spell zilch. It takes human intervention to make a decision, and those interventions at NAVSSES are questionable at best, as is witnessed by the way the place operates. The funny part about the way the place operates is like it's on high speed; at least all the managers I ever worked for were obsessed with speed in some form. I need that pie chart, I need that bar graph, I need, I need, and I need. NAVSEA/NAVSSES should be labeled a bakery from all the pie charts they produce verses tangible goods. In the meantime, ships that request assistance get placed at the bottom of pile of paperwork in the hopes that it will go away, because frankly, so called engineers were often too frightened to make a decision or worse.

Trash collecting lay off:
Minimum wage earners like the janitors were let go from daily work to once a week office trash pickup in order to save the salaries of overstuffed pockets of NAVSSES employees. At one time, places like the shipyard required a lot of engineers, but let's face it, the major world wars have been long over. And much of the shipbuilding is now done by the private yards. If I were the mayor of Philadelphia, I would have something to say about cutting out minimum wage earners, otherwise – what exactly does NAVSSES provide to help the city? The majority of the NAVSSES employees do not live in the city, they live everywhere else but...

What are the Captains next move to save expenses? Have the employee carry their own once a week trash to the dumpsters before going home? Maybe, save even more by doing away with the dumpster and have each employee take it home?

PATENTS

Many of the patents the Navy presently professes to own are somewhat questionable. And I say that, because the majority of their so-called patents are hardly ever requested for by the private industry. What good is a patent if no one else cares to use it? Get what I mean?

Now on the other hand, when I was coming up with some really neat ideas, I asked the Navy's patent expert or headman for advice on filing. I also requested suggestions for how my patent should be written. They sent me a copy of a patent written some time in the 1950s. So that is what I used as my format. What did I know? When I sent my first idea in for a patent–naturally it was shot down. The patent writing format had changed. Great, now I have to pay to resend in all my work and redo it all.

Noticed, that I requested the Navy's help from the expert. I believe his name was Forester. What a joke he was. Six patents later, and he still never ever bothered to provide me with the right information on filing for a patent. I knew it–he was a typical jealous engineer too, just like all of the supervisors and managers I ever worked under at NAVSSES. I was able to get my patents without the Navy's supposedly expert assistance. And that is typical of many of the people in management I had to deal with while working for the Navy. One jealous ass hole after another–that was some of the typical people in management. Just remember, if you have any thoughts of working for the Navy, don't expect to get any recognition for a job well done, promotions are only awarded to those individuals that put up a fight, file grievances or file a lawsuit is a definite plus to getting promoted.

INVENTIVE IDEAS

The Navy rarely rewarded inventive ideas, unless a slew of comrades including the supervisor were mentioned in the patent application. Oh sure, the person who came up with the idea receives a copy of the patent, but so do a dozen others in his group. Another misdeed often perpetrated by the organization, was to strip the inventor of his idea or concept, and hand it to someone else unfamiliar with the project concept. They might as well have given the idea to the janitor. Needless to say, the other person often failed miserably in carrying out what might have been a great invention. Then you might ask; why would the inventor care to submit another great idea under those circumstances? Each and every invention NAVSSES applied for had some other person's suppository fingered crap smeared on it. Proud, maybe somewhat, certainly not as proud, as I was applying for patents on my own.

In this day and age when all sorts of high tech software exist for the engineering arena, it is sad to note that few if any civilians working for the Navy use them. While technology keeps migrating offshore, the Navy has remained stagnant in churning out engineering excellence. Navy patents are phony at best. I know so because you can apply for a patent for just about anything, including the direction a wrench turns. Patents that the Navy claims have benefited the public are typically not so, but instead, major Navy hired contractors like Martin and such do provide such beneficial patents that the public can use.

GOVERNOR VALVES

Since I'm on the subject of travels, I would like to mention some work in San Diego that I performed on the aircraft carrier, the USS Kitty Hawk. I was the project manager on an extensive project to overhaul all the high-pressure steam governors in the four engine rooms. These valves were part of the governing systems for the ship's main propulsion system. A total of sixteen governor valves required overhauling. When I was initially assigned to the huge project, it involved every naval ship class that used steam for propulsion. The original manufacturer of the governors for all these ships had designed specific governor valves for each class of ship. In total, there must have been eighty-five different configurations of the valves. After noting the vast complex number of components, I went about redesigning the whole system to entail only a half dozen valve configurations. Anyone of the steam propulsion ships should be able to adapt one of my valve designs. My new configurations reduced the huge inventory of repair parts the Navy was keeping, as well as the number of repair and technical manuals, logistics and more.

Needless to say, the original manufacturer of the governor valves was furious with my new designs, due to monetary loss. At one point, some engineers in Washington asked me; to explain what I found was wrong with the original designed valves, and to follow it up with a Congressional hearing. There were way too many problems with the original valves too numerous to mention them here. I told the engineers at Washington, that it wasn't necessary to have a hearing, since my new designs had basically knocked the OEM out of the bidding to supply future governor valves.

Anyway, for a year or so, I was traveling from shipyard to shipyard overseeing the reconstruction of the governor valves. My biggest challenge was on the USS Kitty Hawk docked in San Diego. This ship required sixteen valves replaced. My co-assistant from the propulsion division in Philly was Frank Walken, a big Black guy. At the work site, he kept complaining about his knees; so I suggested he remain in our rental car while I did what had to be done on the ship. He was going to sit in the car listening to music, and he would leave briefly to checkout a local computer store. At the time I was working with Frank, he was shopping for the latest MAC computer. I didn't mind him leaving the work site, because in my opinion, he was basically an imbecile, when it came to understanding the governors. It was best Frank not get in my way, rather than he slow me down trying to explain everything to him.

Three days later, the ship's crew informed me that they had to leave the following morning for a few days for maneuvers. I was locked into having to ride the ship, if I was going to complete the work. I took my luggage on board and they put me up in quarters directly below the flight deck. My co-worker returned home. I was somewhat shanghaied to ride the ship. One after another, I dismantled and replaced the governor parts from one engine room to another. At times, I found myself standing in knee-deep water making adjustments to a high pressure steam driven pumps, all the while I was getting burned from the hot steam pipes. Here's a tidbit of information about some of the pieces of trash that might be floating in the bilges; condoms, that's right, every once in a while, I would see one floating in the bilges. You have to wonder what some of the sailors were up to.

In the evening, jet planes took off and landed directly above my cabin. The arresting cable was encased in a pipe running through my room. So, every time, one of the jets hooked itself to my cable, I would hear it rattling in and out of its reel. After a couple days, I got used to the sound and slept through it unfazed.

Working in the engine room is not the area to be in should anything go wrong. I heard about one ship that had one of the steam valves come apart. It killed everyone inside the engine room. It seems someone had substituted brass bolts for toughened steel bolts. Under high pressure, the valve blew apart filling the room instantly with extremely high temperature steam. One of the sailors I spoke with described, how he volunteered to remove his dead fellow mates. Every part of the steamed bodies he touched, fell off in chunks like over cooked chicken in a pressure cooker. The bodies swelled beyond recognition, and eyes bulge out and enlarge to golf ball size protruding beyond the skull. The sailor mentioned that the cream textured bodies were shoveled into large galvanized trashcans, taken from the mess deck. Was he telling the truth, I only know what I was told?

For some odd reasons, I always felt that if something like that happened while I was working down in the engine room, I would be ready to run for the exit. I was kidding myself. A steam blast is instant. Sadly, the engine room operators are no where, no way, rewarded like the officers that spend much of their time under ideal conditions in the upper decks. And yet, the Navy seeks to place more credence and value on officers, who take zero risks and do very little good for the ship, except look professional. In other words, a ship could have ten or twenty officers, but you can bet-cha that only one or two of the officers make all the important or creative decisions.

So where was I, oh yes? I was riding the aircraft carrier replacing the governor valves one after another on the high-pressure steam turbine pumps. All the while, I was getting burnt and bumping my head here and there. I had all four-engine rooms purring when the ship finally docked a couple of weeks later back in San Diego. It was about 11:00pm and dark outside. A crowd of family members was there to greet some of the sailors as I made my way, through the mass of people. I was lugging my big travel luggage suitcase, a heavy box of repair parts, and a toolbox full of miscellaneous. Ok, where is there a taxi, a bus, or anything. There was none, I'll have to walk to the main gate if I want to get a cab. It was around 12:00pm and everything seemed closed. I looked around for a phone to make a call. There was none that I could see, and even if there was, what number do I call for a cab? I reached in my pocket for change and came up with 7 cents in change, great. Cars parked around the ship were leaving for home. The walking, dragging and carrying my stuff seemed endless. My arms were just about to give out. And then, there in the distance was the main gate. I parked my stuff and walked over to ask the guard about getting a cab.

"Just hang out over there, and one will show up."

I sat on an open bench trying to make out the stars in the sky, and two hours later a cab appeared. By the time I was in my hotel room, it was around 4:00am. The next morning without much sleep, I made arrangements for the next flight home. Everything went well with my governor change over project, and I went on to do similar installs on other classes of ships.

And then one day, the manager of the department in charge of propulsion at NAVSSES decided that since this was their section of expertise, that they should get the funding from Washington to oversee the governor repairs. What a big mistake that was. So I was taken off the governor project, and the Black co-worker that was with me on the USS Kitty Hawk's job was put in charge.

Well, it wasn't long before the Hawk carrier was experiencing problems with the governors. Frank, The Black Engineer, was ordered back out to San Diego, to see if he could fix what was ailing the ship. He went there and came back reporting to his boss that Lueder had messed everything up on the governors. "Lueder," he said, "Didn't know what he was doing, and that he wasn't able to fix the ships problems." He suggested they put back everything the way they were. And of course there was much finger pointing, but the technical incompetent Frank would not admit that he knew nothing about how the governors operated. Tomlin, the supervisor in charge of the group refused to allow me to visit the ship to fix what was ailing it.

Finally, after the ship sent out several messages attacking the propulsion department for not fixing their problem, the department manager in charge of the propulsion governors came around to their senses and asked me to help them. At a meeting with various supervisors, and some engineers, the manager in charge of the propulsion system admitted that I alone should handle all matters regarding the steam governors with my fix.

What were they thinking? I even wrote five technical manuals on the subject. No one else understood how the units operated. They all relied on the manufacturer to bail them out whenever they had a problem and these were all engineers. Finally, after three months of bickering about who should be in charge, I was allowed to return to the ship, to repair my creditability of my redesigned high pressure steam governor systems.

I returned to the carrier ship and put back everything the way it should work with my design. I got the carrier's main machinery purring again. I then held a training session with the ship's force and with a couple of mechanics from the local navy repair facility. Upon returning to my office, no one ever said anything positive, no outstanding award, not even a letter of appreciation, nothing. As usual over time, I saw other co-workers do simple jobs at

NAVSSES and receive huge monetary awards for outstanding work, for what amounted to a false phony award.

Engineers were more often awarded monetary accolades as a prelude to their up coming promotions. It was all phony. NAVSSES has a mechanical technician complex, that says that they can't and won't admit that technicians were and are much more knowledgeable in repairing Naval ships and such. It's not the other way around, as the NAVSSES brainy management department believes; that a piece of college paper is more intelligent in resolving ships problems. Many of the engineers feigned illness in the hopes that some other individual would get selected to go check out a ship with mechanical problems. One manager in particular, eventually became our branch head for our MACHALT department. That feigning illness information was per a close Polish friend of mine by the name of Dan. Last names omitted.

Prior to heading out to the carrier ship, my supervisor had asked me if I wanted to have Frank, the Black engineer tag along. After hearing my story of how he helped out before and then receiving overtime for sitting in his car everyday—my boss understood. I told him that I doubted the Black guy even boarded the ship when he was sent out alone, because he didn't understand the system. And another thing I said to my boss; no one from San Diego was there to pick me up when the ship docked around eleven o'clock at night. I went on to tell him how I walked the long distance carry heavy equipment and my suitcase to the main gate. I had to make many stops before I got to the main gate. I also mentioned all the long hours I put in to make everything right onboard. Not a single person from our outfit in San Diego was there to pick me up once the ship docked. It was as if for going out of my way to ride the ship, getting steam burned installing new equipment, and not a single person gave a damn. That was typical of the way Navy managers often cared about their hard workers at NAVSSES. However, if you had a piece of paper—oh well, step right here—I have your promotion, and here is an outstanding award for just showing up for work.

Managers get their promotion from all the nice work we did—you would think that they would have taken better care of the subordinate people. In this case, my manager knew that I designed the new governor system, plus I wrote five technical manuals on the subject and much more saving the Navy millions. Not even an outstanding award or a letter of appreciation did I ever receive. A few guys during ship checks were savvy enough to rub shoulders with the ships captain or the ship's engineering officer, and then get one of them to send out a message of appreciation. Often the message was already written for the officers, and all the ships officers had to do were to make minor changes to the message. I just never felt I had to stoop so low to get recognized for my work. And since this is my story, and I never received credit as author and engineer on the drawings and for writing the five governor technical manuals, I'm going to mention their titles now for historical records, they were the Terry Turbine Governor Valve/Governor Pilot Turbine Models/ Type BWSVG, BFSCS, BWSVG, BHSVG and BPSVG.

What I just covered is one of many such stories where my work away from home base, far exceeded anything that I witnessed others doing to receive an award or a promotion at NAVSSES. I suppose when you're outstanding in what you do, a system like that at NAVSSES turns a blind eye much like ignoring a well running watch. When the watch stops keeping time, we tend to go that extra care to make sure it continues to work, hence the awards to the less than capable.

BUY OUTS TO RETIRE

Buy outs was a nice way of rewarding many of the hard working employees with many years of service, while allowing the Navy to reduce its workforce, thereby reducing operating expense. But in reality, much of it was doled out unfairly based on you social standing with your supervisor and or manager. For example; if your manager wanted to get rid of someone, he would move that person into a non-productive section, thereby ensuring that the person could qualify for the Buy Out of $25,000. You didn't necessarily need to be in a non-productive status to qualify for the bonus; the supervisor just had to say that a specific person was non-productive to receive the bonus. That was a nice going away present wouldn't you say?

Now if you were a hard working person, productive sort of speak, who happen to want to retire because of time served and such, well - the Navy made sure that you were punished by denying you the Buy Out 25K bonus. Fair – I think not. I was one of them.

And then there were the wieners that could weasel their way into the Captain's office, and tell him/her a sad story about family or personal sickness and thereby clinch the retirement bonus. Many of them didn't even come close to having 40 years of service, which you would think, that this fact alone should qualify you for the 25k bonus. As a matter of fact, there was a husband and wife team working at NAVSSES that did just that, play the sickness trump card, and retired with a hefty combined buy out of $50K.

And, and, and I'm not even going to mention nepotism at NAVSSES, where the last time I looked there were thirty plus couples, who were married or related. Related, whereby one or the other relative received favorable treatment. Brothers bringing onboard a high school brother non-competitively and getting him quickly promoted to a GS-12 position, sans any previous technical experience, college education - zip nothing. How fair was that to Joe Public? How fair was that to the shop workers or the students that did pay to attend a technical school? Nepotism is what allowed select individuals to receive that Engineer Equivalent degree, which I was denied.

RETIRE COLA

Yep, the Navy doesn't mention that once you retire the cost living in a specific area, COLA, does not apply. And they do not mention that a good portion of your retirement is lost to survivor's benefits. At forty plus years which included sick leave, I was suppose to receive roughly 76% of my pay, which at the time was close to $90,000 for top step GS-12. $90,000 x .75 = $67,500. Instead I'm getting far less baring Federal Taxes etc. It's more like $55,000.

What about business giants like Bill Gates, here was a guy that never completed college either. At NAVSSES there were lots of great talented people who were over looked at every turn. Overall working for NAVSSES was disappointing in the sense that we were all responsible working adults. And as such why all the chiefs, and or the disproportionate number of pay scales when everyone was working at the same level? To claim, that responsible working employees require a chain of people, telling them what to do, or to ensure that the work is being done seems silly and ridiculous, considering not much constructively is presently being achieved as it stands today in 2008.

The place is so disorganized; like a multi-headed snake flopping about in the grass in search of NAVSEA to force-feed it with funding from time to time. If anything per my opinion, NAVSSES has become an organization run by a bunch of dishonest crooks.

It takes a long time for the so-called state of the art military to advance in technology. As an example, just look at the private industry that discovered the benefits of electrical ship propulsions systems, long before the Navy would adapt to using them. I can site many more such examples of the Navy lagging behind instead of leading the industry in discoveries. NAVSSES is not...

IN CLOSING

In closing I like to say that I was cheated out of a GS-13 promotion. I was cheated out of a multitude of awards for outstanding work performances, for having an excellent attendance, for authoring five technical manuals, for designing a solid state aircraft fueling system for the carriers, plus many more accomplishments too many to list. And I was exploited and cheated out of all the extra schooling I took, and I was cheated out of the SIP retirement monies. NAVSSES management lied and was dishonest to me from the day I set foot in the place. I made just as much effort, if not more, in getting a higher education as a papered engineer, plus I had tons of hands on experience as a toolmaker, not to mention my years in the Design Division of ship building. Corruption and dishonesty at NAVSSES is unsurpassed and the place is long over due for investigation. Hopefully, those remaining will not be victimized too by the fictitious disorder mentality presently running the place. And for the directors, managers and supervisors that retired prior to the book being published – you too were part of the scandalous behavior, which I write about.

Now to point out some of the violations I mentioned in the beginning regarding public service and the standards of conduct guide, here we go:

Under don't use nonpublic information to benefit yourself or anyone else.

What do you call all the NAVSSES employees that retired and immediately returned to work as contractors while using the same office space they originally worked in?

What do you call contracting NAVSSES employees retiring and returning to favor the same contractor they happen to be working for?

What do you call hiring contractor employees to work for NAVSSES non-competitively?

Don't use Federal property for unauthorized purposes.

What do you call setting up your own convenience store and running it during working hours? Fund raising for parties – I think not.

Don't take jobs or hold financial interests that conflict with your Government responsibilities.

What do you call allowing contractors to use government space for their offices? Or running a business from work.

Don't take actions that give the appearance that they are illegal or unethical.

What do you call burning up funds at the end of fiscal years to ensure more funding the following year?

What do you call questionable $7000 plus awards for creating pie charts?

What do you call targeting technicians as inferior workers too dumb to qualify for many of the promotions?

What do you call managers that take trips solely for vacation time and or for personal monetary travel gain?

What do you call managers that promote the inexperienced right out of school children to managerial positions over – well you know…

Rule under Gifts. You may not give, make a donation, or solicit a gift for someone superior to you in the chain of command.

What do you call someone, who was promoted to a GS-13 supervisor position after purchasing the manager's house?

Under Conflicts of Interest. You may not do government work on a particular matter that will affect the financial interest of any family member.

Boy, where do I start? Look, there are brothers helping brothers get promoted and husband and wife teams, not to mention the orgy of love affairs.

Commercial Dealings Between DoN Employees. You may not solicit sales to junior grade personnel.

What do you call setting up a convenience store by a GS-12 and 13, and sanctioned by a GS-14? And what about asking a subordinate to buy your residence prior to receiving a promotion?

And there's more…

If you ever decide to go to work for a place like NAVSSES, I suggest that you make yourself known from day one. Don't even think of humbling yourself to anyone, because humbling means you are someone to be walked on. By that I mean holler for everything, even if that means e-mailing the captain everyday. Just remember to keep bugging the captain and director until you get what you want and deserve. Otherwise, if you try to rely on your supervisors or manager to help you to get advanced - don't hold your sphincter/breath. The Navy will not throw out a life preserver to save your ass in the business world, because it's every person for them selves. It's the way the place is organized and structured. There is no oversight, they do what they want until the union steps in, or someone hires an attorney.

There is no longer an institute of honesty, integrity or a safe place to work at NAVSSES and other such military civilian run places. Just like Enron, AIG, the housing collapse and so, it's big businesses that are proving to the rest of the world, that even our top leaders like President Clinton, are all crooks with zip scruples. NAVSSES believe me when I say, was and is no different. Without checks and balances who is watching over the Captains or the directors? Like I said, "If you want to gage how well a supervisor or manager is doing in an organization, ask the subordinates and or the contractors."

And one last word to the newly promoted warehouse keeper from a GS-12 to GS-13, I congratulated you for being promoted before I left. When things backup in the warehouse because the place has been whittled down to a handful of people, don't be accusing the employees of taking handfuls of project components for personal usage, for why you are behind in your work or can't get projects shipped. I for one rarely if ever visited the warehouse during my last five years at NAVSSES.

Hopefully, this book will bring closure to the many such abused victims and allow them to move on.

President Reagan said, "Trust, but verify."

2189172

Made in the USA